COOL CAREERS WITHOUT COLLEGE FOR
PEOPLE
WHO LOVE
SPORTS

COOL CAREERS WITHOUT COLLEGE FOR
PEOPLE
WHO LOVE
SPORTS

ADAM B. HOFSTETTER

The Rosen Publishing Group, Inc., New York

To Sarah

Published in 2007 by The Rosen Publishing Group, Inc.
29 East 21st Street, New York, NY 10010

Library of Congress Cataloging-in-Publication Data

Hofstetter, Adam B.
Cool careers without college for people who love sports by Adam B. Hofstetter.—1st ed.
    p. cm.—(Cool careers without college)
Includes index.
ISBN 1-4042-0749-X (library binding)
1. Sports—Vocational guidance—Juvenile literature. I. Title. II. Series.
GV734.H64 2006
796.023—dc22

                                        2005028740

Manufactured in the United States of America

CONTENTS

INTRODUCTION

OK, so you love sports. You love watching sports, you love playing sports, and you wish there was some way you could have a career working in sports. But how?

You see the professional athletes at the top of their games, and you see the money they make, the exciting lifestyles they lead, and the glory and adoration they earn by excelling on the field of play. But only a tiny percentage of athletes have the talent to play at the highest levels of their sport. What about the rest of us? Is there any way that regular people can turn their love of sports into a career?

The professional athletes may get all the media attention, but there are plenty of other ways to make sports pay the bills. From the scouts who sign the players to professional contracts to the umpires and referees who make the calls on the field to the cameramen and photographers who record it all, there are hundreds of people working behind the scenes at every sporting event.

Watch baseball games from the press box as an official scorer. Dance on the basketball court as a team mascot. Nurture the playing field as a groundskeeper. Share mementos from the game's greatest moments with other fans as a memorabilia dealer. These and the many other careers described in this book will allow you not just to make money but also to live your dreams and play an active role in the games and events you love. And best of all, by transforming your passion into a profession, you'll be able to do what you enjoy every day. This book will give you some ideas about careers in the field you love: sports.

1

SCOUT

Most people think of scouting as getting paid to watch games all day. There's certainly some truth to that, but scouts are some of the hardest workers in sports. In addition to a keen eye for talent and a thorough knowledge of the game, scouts need self-discipline and perseverance to handle the challenges of life as a scout and help

Scouts from many National Football League (NFL) teams watch and time a college football player as he runs through speed drills at the University of Nebraska in Lincoln. Scouts often travel a great deal in order to observe and report on hundreds of athletes.

their teams determine which players to pursue and which to avoid.

Description

Scouts must know how to recognize and evaluate a player's talent. Specific job duties depend on the sport and the level and type of scout. Some scouts search the country for talented amateur players. Others evaluate professional players on opposing teams before trades or free-agent signings. Still

others live in foreign countries and seek out the best international talent. But the basic duties never change: a scout's job is to find players, evaluate them, and, in many cases, sign them to contracts.

Travel is a big part of the job. Most scouts are assigned to specific regions, but even so, a scout will frequently spend as much time traveling between games as watching them. To keep tabs on players and evaluate their skills, professional scouts sometimes watch several games a day. As well as attending games, being a scout includes visiting schools or teams and keeping on top of any school, league, or regional events—such as tournaments—that may feature prospects. That means long drives, cheap motels to cut down on expenses, and time away from home.

There's also an administrative side to scouting. Scouts give their bosses detailed reports on which players will be able to help the team and how. They file paperwork on every prospect and must be organized enough to make sure they're covering their assigned region thoroughly and completely.

As you might imagine, building relationships is essential to being a good scout. Scouts talk to players and their families, and to coaches. Amateur scouts in particular need to maintain relationships with schools and leagues in their regions so they can be the first to find out about potential superstars.

Good scouts also have to think positively and be assertive. They might be called on to defend their evaluation

Future American League MVP Alex Rodriguez fields a call from the Seattle Mariners telling him that they've just made him the first pick in baseball's 1993 amateur draft. Rodriguez was scouted by dozens of major league teams before being drafted.

of a player or help negotiate his or her contract. Scouts are often giving a young player and that player's family their first impression of a particular team. That means scouts must always be professional, both in appearance and behavior.

Scouting work itself can be a lot of fun, but, as the scouts who were the first to evaluate Alex Rodriguez, Peyton Manning, or LeBron James would probably tell you, the biggest satisfaction comes when one of the players you've recommended makes an impact for the team you work for.

Education and Training

There's no set career path to follow and no license or degree you need to obtain to become a scout. Many scouts have played or coached professionally, but that's certainly not the only way to get into this line of work. The Major League Baseball Scouting Bureau runs a ten-day "scout school" every

Scout Specifics

Professional teams have a variety of scouting jobs.

- **Amateur scouts** evaluate amateur players. Their recommendations help determine which players a team will select in the annual amateur draft.
- **Minor league scouts** evaluate players in the minor leagues. They look for players whom their team might be interested in acquiring through trades.
- **Major league scouts** concentrate on the major leagues. They look for players to acquire via trades and free agency.
- **Advance scouts** are sent to study an opposing team several days before a game or series of games. They watch the players' performances and look for strengths or weaknesses that might prove useful to know when playing against them.

autumn. Attending this boot camp is not necessary, but it certainly helps. Well over half of the students who have been through the camp are working in baseball in some capacity, including the school's most famous graduate: current Chicago White Sox general manager Ken Williams. Online scouting courses for football, baseball, or basketball—taught by former scouts in each sport—are available through a company called Sports Management Worldwide.

The best way to get started in the field is to get to know the high school and college players and coaches in your hometown. Then track down a scout who covers your area. That scout can help you get started as an associate scout. This is usually an unpaid part-time position where you will make use of your knowledge of the area to help the scout cover his or her territory more thoroughly and effectively.

As you become more experienced in player evaluations and scouting reports, and have some contact with a team's scouting director, you can move up to paid part-time work and eventually become a full-time area scout. Area scouts are responsible for covering their assigned regions, which typically encompass at least two neighboring states. With a record of success, an area scout can move up to area supervisor, where he or she will oversee all the area scouts in an even larger region. From there, you can move up to national cross-checker, where you'll collect scouting reports for the top players and assess their talents to make sure the reports are accurate and consistent. The most successful scouts advance to become scouting directors, and many move into other administrative positions in the team's front office. Some even start their own independent scouting services.

Jay Weitzel, the Northeast scout for the Minnesota Twins, addresses hopeful players during an open tryout in New Britain, Connecticut, in July 2005. Senior scouts are being assigned to oversee increasingly larger geographic areas.

Salary

The U.S. Department of Labor's Bureau of Labor Statistics groups scouts together with coaches and says that their median annual salary was $32,260 in 2004. Most of those earned between $17,890 and $42,250 a year. The scouts with salaries in the bottom 10 percent, mostly part-timers, earned less than $13,370, and those in the highest 10 percent earned more than $60,230.

Outlook

Every professional sports team has a multitude of scouts in various positions across the country and around the world. Though every team has a different budget, most teams have at least twenty scouts on staff. Many colleges and universities with high-profile athletic programs employ scouts to find and recruit high school players. Some professional leagues have central scouting bureaus (such as the Major League Scouting Bureau) that employ scouting staffs. Football and basketball in particular have many independent scouting services that offer scouting reports and other draft-related information to National Football League (NFL) or National Basketball Association (NBA) teams and news organizations.

Because many scouts stay in their jobs for decades, competition for openings can be tough. However, as sports becomes a more global industry, the need for international scouts will continue to rise. Moreover, several teams have dipped into foreign markets in recent years without being fully prepared and have been hurt by costly free-agent busts like Kazuo Matsui of the New York Mets. Those highly publicized mistakes have taught teams how vital it is to have good scouts abroad.

FOR MORE INFORMATION

ORGANIZATIONS

Major League Scouting Bureau (MLSB)
3500 Porsche Way, Suite 100
Ontario, CA 91764
(909) 980-1881
   The official scouting bureau of Major League Baseball.

WEB SITES

Major League Baseball
http://mlb.mlb.com/NASApp/mlb/mlb/news/mlb_news.jsp?ymd=20
   030211&content_id=199087&vkey=news_mlb&fext=.jsp
   This section of Major League Baseball's Web site includes an interview with the director of the Major League Scouting Bureau and a
   twelve-part series chronicling a reporter's experience at one of the
   MLSB's scout schools.

SoccerCareer.com
http://www.soccercareer.com
   Offerings for soccer jobs as well as a career center are provided for
   players, coaches, agents, schools, and scouts.

Sports Management Worldwide
http://www.sportsmanagementworldwide.com
   Sports Management Worldwide offers several eight-week-long
   online courses for people who want to work in sports.

BOOKS

Carree, Chuck. *Scout's Honor: The Life of a Baseball Gentleman.*
Wilmington, NC: Possum Trot Press, 2004.
This book profiles baseball scout Rip Tutor and gives a behind-the-scenes account of life as a professional scout.

Kerrane, Kevin. *Dollar Sign on the Muscle: The World of Baseball Scouting.*
Lincoln, NE: University of Nebraska Press, Bison Books, 1999.
Provides a historical overview of scouting, as well as stories and quotes from dozens of professional scouts.

Murff, Red, and Mike Capps. *The Scout: Searching for the Best in Baseball.* Nashville, TN: W Publishing Group, 1996.
The legendary scout presents a behind-the-scenes look at life as a scout.

Palmer, Joe E. *Old Baseball Scout and His Players.* Beverly Hills, CA: Remlap Publishing Company, 1987.
This book features the anecdotal reminiscences of retired scout Dan Crowley.

Russo, Jim, and Bob Hammel. *Super Scout: Thirty-Five Years of Major League Scouting.* Chicago, IL: Bonus Books, 1992.
A memoir from Jim Russo about his long career as a scout for the Baltimore Orioles.

Shanks, Bill. *Scout's Honor: The Bravest Way to Build a Winning Team.*
Atlanta, GA: Sterling & Ross Publishers, 2005.
Offers insight into the debate between scouts and statisticians over the best way to determine talent, using the Atlanta Braves as a focal point. The book also explains what criteria baseball scouts use to judge talent.

Winegardner, Mark. *Prophet of the Sandlots: Journeys with a Major League Scout.* New York, NY: Atlantic Monthly Press, 1990.
This book chronicles a year with long-time major league scout Tony Lucadello.

2

GROUNDSKEEPER

Making sure fields look their best while being safe for players and consistent from game to game is a demanding but rewarding job. If you like tending lawns, imagine how much more exciting it would be to be a groundskeeper for a professional football or baseball team or a golf course.

Finding and fixing a leak in the sprinkler system at Waterfront Park in Trenton, New Jersey, is all in a day's work for Trenton Thunder groundskeeper Nicole Sherry. Sherry is one of relatively few women who have worked as head groundskeepers for professional baseball teams.

Description

Besides professional stadiums and golf courses, groundskeepers can tend athletic fields for schools and public parks. Regardless of where groundskeepers work, their job is to keep the playing surface clean, beautiful, and functional. They are responsible for keeping the grass or artificial turf in top condition, marking out boundaries such as foul lines or end zones, and even painting turf with team names and logos. Groundskeepers mow, water, fertilize, and aerate the fields, as well as maintain the soil underneath so that it supports the grass and allows for proper drainage.

Baseball team groundskeepers often mow decorative patterns into the field. They are responsible for the upkeep of the infield dirt and pitcher's mound. Before a game and between innings, they rake the dirt smooth and sometimes water it down to prevent dust from blowing into the fielders' eyes. Workers on fields with synthetic turf also vacuum and disinfect the turf after each use. Periodically, they must remove the turf and replace the cushioning pad beneath it. Groundskeepers can often be seen on the field tending to the turf when it rains or snows during games. They also protect and maintain the field during the off-season.

Workers who care for golf courses are called greenskeepers. In addition to many of the things that other groundskeepers do, greenskeepers tend to sand traps and water hazards. Occasionally, they reposition the holes on putting greens to prevent uneven wear of the turf or to adjust the difficulty of the game. Greenskeepers also keep canopies, benches, ball washers, and tee markers repaired and freshly painted. In addition, they clear snow from walkways and parking lots and maintain and repair groundskeeping equipment.

Over time, you can work your way up to a supervisory position such as head groundskeeper. Supervisors and head groundskeepers schedule work for crews based on upcoming events, weather conditions, or equipment availability. They train new workers and might prepare cost estimates or other budgetary reports. They also perform spot checks to ensure quality and are periodically called upon to assist their staff with deadlines (such as having the field ready for a game or other event) or when there are not enough workers.

The work is physically demanding, and groundskeepers need to be in good physical shape. Keep in mind that the work can be repetitive and that it is performed mostly outdoors and in all kinds of weather. Hours can be very long during the season, even when the team is on the road and no games are scheduled. Groundskeepers are always under pressure to get the job done and, unfortunately, they are the first to get criticized if a ball takes a bad bounce or a field is in poor condition.

Education and Training

Usually, there are no minimum educational requirements for entry-level positions. Short-term, on-the-job training is generally the best way to learn how to operate equipment and care for grass and soil. Some vocational high schools offer courses in landscaping as do community colleges and private landscaping associations. A valid driver's license and good driving record can be helpful for jobs that include driving lawn mowers and other vehicles.

Groundskeepers work in all kinds of weather, including snow and frigid temperatures. This groundskeeper shovels snow off the yard lines during a late November game between the NFL's Oakland Raiders and Denver Broncos.

The simplest way to gain some experience and knowledge as a groundskeeper is to work on your own lawn or the lawns of your neighbors. Private golf courses, minor league baseball teams, and city parks departments routinely hire students for summer groundskeeper jobs. Then you can start moving your way up to better courses or higher-level teams.

To move up to supervisory positions, you'll need to demonstrate a willingness to work hard and quickly. You'll also need to have good communication skills. Most head groundskeepers

Greenskeeper Charlie Mott mows the golf course at Green Meadow Country Club in Helena, Montana, in preparation for a tournament. Knowing how to operate several different types of maintenance equipment is important for a groundskeeper.

have some formal landscaping education, such as continuing-education courses in soils, turf-grass management, or other related fields. Once you reach a certain level of training and experience, several professional organizations offer a written exam that will make you a certified groundskeeper. The Professional Grounds Management Society, for example, offers two different levels of certification depending on your education and experience. Although not necessary, certification will help you get better jobs and earn more money.

Salary

Entry-level groundskeepers usually get paid minimum wage. The hourly rate can rise quickly with experience. According to statistics from the U.S. Department of Labor, landscaping and groundskeeping workers averaged about $11.65 an hour in 2004. Supervisors earn much more. A salary survey from 2001 by the Sports Turf Managers Association shows that the top few percent of turf managers earn over $85,000 a year. According to PayScale.com—a Web site that offers salary comparisons for hundreds of jobs—golf course groundskeepers can earn as much as $120,000 annually. On top of their salaries, tenured turf managers can negotiate for extra time off during the off-season and use that time to earn more money as paid turf-care consultants.

Outlook

As with any job in professional sports, positions at the top levels are scarce. However, jobs at the lower levels are plentiful and are expected to continue to increase in the near future. Landscaping and groundskeeping workers held almost 1.2 million jobs in 2002. Because beginners are usually faced with low pay and lots of physical work, many employers have trouble filling openings and then keeping them filled. Expected growth in the construction of parks, golf courses, and stadiums will contribute to the demand for groundskeepers. There are literally thousands of high school, college, and minor league facilities across the United States and Canada, all of which need care and maintenance. There is also a growing trend in which many teams have been replacing their artificial turf with natural grass, which requires more maintenance and usually a larger grounds crew.

FOR MORE INFORMATION

ORGANIZATIONS

Canadian Nursery Landscape Association (CNLA)
RR #4, Station Main
7856 Fifth Street
Milton, ON L9T 2X8
Canada
(905) 875-1399
Web site: http://www.canadanursery.com
> The CNLA is the national umbrella organization for eight provincial member associations in the landscape, horticulture, and nursery industry across Canada. It offers educational programs, news about events and trade shows, employment opportunities, and professional certification.

Golf Course Superintendents Association of America (GCSAA)
1421 Research Park Drive
Lawrence, KS 66049-3859
(800) 472-7878
Web site: http://www.gcsaa.org

The leading professional organization for people who manage and maintain golf courses. Provides members with professional development resources, educational opportunities, and free life insurance. The Web site offers comprehensive industry information, discussion forums, job postings, and other career resources.

Professional Baseball Employment Opportunities (PBEO)

P.O. Box A
St. Petersburg, FL 33731
(866) 937-7236
Web site: http://www.pbeo.com
PBEO is a subsidiary of Minor League Baseball, the governing body of the minor leagues. PBEO provides year-round job placement services to its member clubs and a career network. The organization runs a yearly job fair in conjunction with the Baseball Winter Meetings and has job listings in such categories as stadium operations and field maintenance.

Professional Grounds Management Society (PGMS)

720 Light Street
Baltimore, MD 21230
(800) 609-7467
Web site: http://www.pgms.org
With over 1,200 members worldwide, PGMS is a professional society for institutional grounds managers. PGMS offers industry news, educational programs, and two levels of certification for groundskeepers and grounds managers depending on experience, education, and score on a written exam.

Sports Turf Managers Association

805 New Hampshire, Suite E
Lawrence, KS 66044
(800) 323-3875

Web site: http://www.sportsturfmanager.org
> The organization's Web site offers job postings in addition to information on all aspects of the industry, including research, official field dimensions, and links to Web sites from chapters of the association.

WEB SITES

Green Media Online
http://www.greenmediaonline.com
> An industry portal for information, education, and products.

Landscape Online
http://www.landscapeonline.com
> A top landscape industry site that offers a wide range of information concerning landscape trends, products, and jobs.

The Landscaping & Groundskeeping Expo
http://www.landscapingexpo.net
> The official Web site of Canada's annual landscaping industry trade show.

Pro Garden Biz
http://www.progardenbiz.com
> An online magazine for professional landscapers and groundskeepers, this site presents many techniques and helpful tips, and includes articles about the industry.

BOOKS

Mellor, David R. *The Lawn Bible: Fenway Park's Master Groundskeeper Tells You How to Keep Your Lawn Green, Groomed, and Growing.* New York, NY: Hyperion, 2003.
> This comprehensive, illustrated guide offers lawn-care tips from the head groundskeeper for the Boston Red Sox, as well as anecdotes from his time tending their playing field.

Mellor, David R. *Picture Perfect: Mowing Techniques for Lawns, Landscapes, and Sports.* New York, NY: John Wiley & Sons, 2001. Mellor shares mowing and maintenance secrets. The book includes simple, step-by-step techniques for creating uniquely patterned playing fields and touches on other issues such as grass selection and fertilizers.

PERIODICALS

Golf Course Management
1421 Research Park Drive
Lawrence, KS 60049
(785) 841-2240
Web site: http://www.gcsaa.org
The official magazine of the GCSAA.

Grounds Maintenance
9800 Metcalf Avenue
Overland Park, KS 66212
(913) 967-1758
Web site: http://www.grounds-mag.com
Contains articles on chemicals, equipment, irrigation, and more.

Landscape Management
7500 Old Oak Boulevard
Cleveland, OH 44130
(440) 891-2729
Web site: http://www.landscapemanagement.net
News about green industry issues and all aspects of landscaping.

Lawn & Landscape
4012 Bridge Avenue
Cleveland, OH 44113

Web site: http://www.lawnandlandscape.com
Includes articles on varied topics like weeds, seeds, equipment, and how to manage your own business.

SportsTURF
P.O. Box 280
Dauphin, PA 17018
(717) 805-4197
Web site: http://www.greenmediaonline.com
The official publication of the Sports Turf Managers Association.

Turf
P.O. Box 449
St. Johnsbury, VT 05819
(800) 422-7147
Web site: http://www.turfmagazine.com
A magazine for grounds maintenance managers, golf course managers, and other landscaping professionals.

Turf & Recreation
275 James Street
Delhi, ON N4B 2B2
Canada
(519) 582-8873
Web site: http://www.turfandrec.com
Published seven times a year, including the annual buyers' guide and directory, this magazine serves sports turf managers, golf course superintendents, lawn and landscape contractors, and municipal grounds managers.

3

UMPIRE/ REFEREE

Being an official is one of the most thankless jobs in sports; your mistakes are public and you get bombarded with criticism. It takes intense concentration and a thick skin. But what other job puts you on the field during the game, interacting with the players and coaches?

There are several types of refer-ees in the NFL. Field judges are responsible for ruling on passes that cross the goal line, like this touchdown pass that a St. Louis Rams player caught before flip-ping the ball to the official pictured here.

Description

The basic job of every sports official is to enforce the rules of the game, but knowing the rules is hardly all there is to it. Umpires and referees must be able to uphold a sense of fair-ness, keep order, promote safety, and encourage good sportsmanship. Umpires and referees also keep official records of the game and file reports about any note-worthy incidents, such as arguments with or ejections of players or coaches. They must make instantaneous decisions and resolve con-flicts, all the while dealing with stress and pressure. A good sports official remains practically invisible, handling a lot of authority without abusing or overreaching it.

When nobody knows who officiated the game and you can leave the building unnoticed, you've done your job well.

The job has some physical requirements. It goes without saying that you'll need excellent vision, but being a sports official also requires a great deal of physical activity—you must get yourself in the best position to make the call, and that often means running alongside the players while avoiding getting in the way. Hockey officials also need to be good ice skaters.

Even at the high school level, the key to successful officiating is to be prepared. Officials often arrive at least half an hour before game time to go over possible game scenarios with each other: where to stand during certain types of plays, how much contact to allow, what the coaches tend to complain about, how to control the crowd, and anything else that comes to mind.

In addition to knowing the rules better than everyone else on the field, having an even temperament and good vision, and being physically fit, umpires and referees must be able to concentrate intently throughout the entire game, with no exceptions. "Looking away for even one second can mean missing important action," writes Shelly Field in *Career Opportunities in the Sports Industry*.

Umpires and referees are required to travel to all games, whether local or across the country. They visit new and exciting places on a regular basis, but they are away from

their families for extended periods of time and work on weekends, at night, and on holidays. The nature of the job requires officials to be on their feet for most, if not all, of the game. Unless the game is in a domed stadium, baseball and football officials have to work outside no matter how hot, cold, or otherwise unpleasant the weather may be. However, there's little preparation before each game and work hours are short since games last only about three hours. Officials have many months off when the season ends, and major league umpires even get paid time off during the season.

Education and Training

Education and training is very different for baseball umpires than it is for other sports officials. To become an official in most sports, a sound knowledge of the rule book is the only schooling you'll need. Most officials start out as part-timers in youth and recreational leagues. You can contact your local YMCA/YWCA or your town's parks and recreation department for information on leagues and any officiating organizations in your area. As you learn the ropes and

The toughest part of a hockey official's job is to stay close to the action and make accurate calls while making sure not to interfere with play. Acrobatics are often the result, as NHL referee Stephen Walkom demonstrates in a game between the New Jersey Devils and the Anaheim Mighty Ducks.

develop your skills, you'll be able to work middle school and high school games. Your state high school association can put you in touch with the right people. College referees must be certified by an officiating school and be evaluated during a trial period. Some larger college conferences have other requirements, such as residence within the conference boundaries along with previous experience that typically includes several years officiating at high school, community college, or other smaller college conference games. In major college programs, officials are "scouted" by assigners or league commissioners, and the very best of them get the final call to the professional leagues.

At the top levels, the requirements get much more strict. The NFL, for example, requires its officials to have at least ten years of experience, with at least five years spent at the collegiate or minor professional level. Candidates get thorough background checks from the NFL's security department and screenings by clinical psychologists to determine intelligence and the ability to handle stress. Usually, there is also a comprehensive test on the league's rules and an interview with a panel from the NFL's officiating department. The National Hockey League (NHL) has official training schools and camps, but also suggests gaining experience at lower levels. The Association of Boxing Commissions (ABC) puts all boxing officials through their own certification program and strongly recommends that officials attend an association-approved training seminar every year.

Practicing making calls is just part of the five-week training that students receive at officially sanctioned schools like the Jim Evans Academy of Professional Umpiring, shown here. Prospective umpires also spend many hours in the classroom studying Major League Baseball's extensive rulebook.

Being a baseball umpire is, well, a whole different ball game. If you plan to umpire in high schools or colleges, follow the same career path as the officials in other sports: start small in little leagues or corporate leagues and work your way up. But if your goal is to umpire in the major leagues someday, you must take a different route.

In addition to fulfilling professional baseball's basic requirements of a high school diploma, 20/20 vision (with or without glasses or contact lenses), good communication skills, and quick reflexes, prospective umpires need to attend a professional umpire training school. In the United States, there are currently two schools whose curricula have been approved by the Professional Baseball Umpires Corporation (PBUC): the Harry Wendelstedt Umpire School and the Jim Evans Academy of Professional Umpiring. (Both schools are run by former major league umpires.) Only the very best graduates of each school move on to the next step—the Umpire Evaluation Course, an advanced camp run by the PBUC. The PBUC then assigns the top umpires to the lowest levels of the minor leagues.

Umpires can spend anywhere from seven to twelve years in the minors before even being considered for a major league job. Umpires who aren't promoted to the next level every two years are usually expected to leave. If that becomes the case, your professional training and minor league experience can help you get jobs officiating college games. At the AAA level (the highest level of the minor leagues), umpires get three years to impress Major League Baseball's (MLB's) executive umpiring staff before they get tossed out. Top AAA umpires are picked to serve as reserves for the majors, which means they'll work major league games when major league umpires get sick or go on vacation. Those reservists are usually the first to be offered jobs in the majors when one opens up.

Salary

A sports official's salary depends on the sport and level of competition. For part-timers, pay is usually per game. For example, in one suburb north of New York City, high school basketball officials get paid about $90 per game. Median annual earnings of sports officials were $20,540 in 2002. The highest 10 percent—all full-timers—earned more than $40,350. Minor league umpires currently earn $1,800–$2,000 per month at the lowest levels, gradually increasing to $2,500–$3,400 per month in class AAA. The league also pays for health and life insurance and hotels, and AAA umpires are usually provided with paid rental cars. Umpires can earn additional money by being selected to work the All-Star Game and playoff games for their level of the minors. They can also work during the off-season in winter leagues. Women's National Basketball League (WNBA) referees earn about $500 per game, which works out to $16,000 for a thirty-two-game season.

Salaries climb significantly for those who make it to the top levels. NFL officials work only sixteen regular-season games and are considered part-time employees, but they still get paid anywhere from $25,000 to $70,000 per year. NBA referees earn anywhere from $90,000 to $225,000 annually. NHL rookie officials earn a $115,000 annual salary, and fifteen-year veterans make up to $220,000 a year. Major

League Baseball umpires do even better, starting at $90,000 a year and going up to $350,000 for the most tenured. They also receive good benefits, a pension, and first-class travel expenses. And if that's not enough, major league umpires get another $17,500 if they're chosen to work the playoffs, as well as $20,000 for the World Series.

Outlook

From archery to volleyball, officials are needed throughout the United States and Canada at every level of competition. The U.S. Department of Labor expects jobs for sports officials to increase by 10 to 20 percent through the year 2012. Youth and corporate leagues mainly hire part-timers. Opportunities for part-time officials at the high school level are also plentiful. There are jobs at the college and semi-professional level, though competition can be stiff. A job officiating at the top level of any sport is difficult to obtain. For example, there are 225 umpires working in the minor leagues, but only 68 in the majors. However, somebody must be on the field making the calls; with talent and hard work, that somebody can be you.

> Violet Palmer became the first woman to referee a regular-season game for any all-male professional sports league when she officiated an NBA game between the Vancouver Grizzlies and Dallas Mavericks on October 31, 1997.

FOR MORE INFORMATION

ORGANIZATIONS

International Association of Approved Basketball Officials
12321 Middlebrook Road, Suite 290
P.O. Box 1300
Germantown, MD 20875-1300
(301) 540-5180
Web site: http://www.iaabo.org
> With roughly 200 local chapters, this professional organization for basketball referees offers training and education.

National Association of Sports Officials (NASO)
2017 Lathrop Avenue
Racine, WI 53405
(262) 632-5448
Web site: http://www.naso.org
> An organization for officials of all levels and sports. Its Web site offers information on officiating, including links to local and national associations.

National Federation of State High School Associations (NFHS)
P.O. Box 690
Indianapolis, IN 46206
(317) 972-6900
Web site: http://www.nfhs.org
> Contact the NFHS for information on officiating high school baseball, softball, football, basketball, and soccer games.

The Professional Baseball Umpire Corporation (PBUC)
P.O. Box A
St. Petersburg, FL 33731
(727) 456-1722
Web site: http://www.minorleaguebaseball.com
  The PBUC trains and evaluates all umpires in the minor league baseball system.

SCHOOLS

There are two umpire schools accepted by Major League Baseball:

Harry Wendelstedt Umpire School
88 South St. Andrews Drive
Ormond Beach, FL 32174
(386) 672-4879
Web site: http://www.umpireschool.com

Jim Evans Academy of Professional Umpiring
12741 Research Boulevard, Suite 401
Austin, TX 78759
(512) 335-5959
Web site: http://www.umpireacademy.com

WEB SITES

Baseball Umpires
http://www.baseballumpires.com
  This Web site for professional umpires offers links to official rules of the game, FAQs, and a newsletter.

Major League Baseball.com
http://www2.mlb.com/NASApp/mlb/mlb/official_info/mlb_umpires.jsp
  The umpire section of the MLB site includes information on rules of the game and biographies of current major league umpires. Be sure to check out the overview of how to become an umpire.

National Association of Sports Officials (NASO): How to Become an Official

http://www.naso.org/BeOfficial/bofficial.htm

> This section of the NASO site provides information about how to get started as a sports official.

National Hockey League Officials Association

http://www.nhlofficials.com

> The Web site for the union of NHL officials offers information on becoming a hockey official, NHL rules, and more.

The Official Call

http://www.tjhsst.edu/~jleaf/writing/top_oc.htm

> A discussion of college and professional football rules and their application.

Start Officiating

http://start.officiating.com

> Offers detailed instructions on how to start a career as a sports official.

BOOKS

Childress, Carl. *Behind the Mask.* Franksville, WI: Referee Enterprises, 1987.
> This book, along with the author's *The Umpire's Answer Book* (1987) and *Take Charge! Baseball Umpiring* (1992) are widely considered to be essential reading for umpires.

Demetriou, George. *Judgment Calls: A Football Officiating Philosophy.* Franksville, WI: Referee Enterprises, 2003.
> Offers practical and thoughtful guidance on many of the gray areas in football officiating, in which judgment plays as big a part as the rule book.

Demetriou, George, and Bill Topp. *Smart Baseball Umpiring: How to Get Better Every Game.* Franksville, WI: Referee Enterprises, 1999.
> Discusses mechanics, useful methods for analyzing your performance, and advice on how to admit your mistakes without undermining your authority.

Field, Shelly. *Career Opportunities in the Sports Industry.* 2nd ed.
New York, NY: Checkmark Books, 1999.
A book that provides advice for becoming an umpire as well as
information on other careers in sports.

Leonhardt, Cheryl. *N.A.P.B.L. Umpire Manual.* Chicago, IL: Triumph
Books, 1998.
This book explains the rules and regulations of being an umpire.

Odums, R. I. *Career Guide to Sports Officiating.* Cleveland, OH:
Guidepost Publishers & Distributors, 1985.
A useful guide to getting your career started. Odums has also written similar books on officiating dozens of sports from archery to
wrestling.

Savage, Jim. *A Career in Professional Sports.* Minneapolis, MN:
Capstone Press, 1996.
Savage's book includes descriptions of several careers relating to
sports, including that of sports official.

PERIODICALS

Referee
P.O. Box 161
Franksville, WI 53126
(262) 632-8855
Web site: http://www.referee.com/
Referee magazine is written by and for sports officials and offers
articles, tips, and information on training.

VIDEOS

You Have to Love It When They Boo!
This twelve-minute video shows what the life of an official is like.
It is available from the National Association of Sports Officials
(NASO) Web site (http://www.naso.org) or by phone (800-733-6100).

4

SCOREBOARD OPERATOR

Maybe you've seen the hand-operated scoreboard relics still used in some baseball parks and thought it would be fun to be one of the people manually posting every hit and run. Or maybe you've watched the high-tech graphics and directives and thought you could do it better. Or perhaps you just like pushing buttons and playing with electronics. If any of these descriptions

Scoreboard operators for high school teams often perform other duties as well. Mark Sanders operates the Minneapolis South High School's scoreboard and also serves as the school's athletic director and public address announcer.

sound like you, you might want to consider a career as a scoreboard operator.

Description

At neighborhood and high school events and at some smaller colleges, operating a scoreboard usually means manipulating a few buttons and switches to update the score and any clocks and timers as the game necessitates. At bigger colleges and in professional leagues, it usually means working on a team of operators who control a main scoreboard, a giant video board, and several auxiliary scoreboards. The professional teams show statistics, graphics, replays, sponsors' commercials, and scores and highlights from other games. They run light and sound shows and orchestrate other scoreboard-related entertainment during the game's downtimes, and they do it all in an effort to entertain and excite tens of thousands of fans.

For example, Giants Stadium—home of the NFL's New York Giants and Jets—in New Jersey's Meadowlands has a team of twenty-one operators to run the building's twelve scoreboards. Crews usually include more than just scoreboard operators. There are technical directors, camera operators, statistics coordinators, and audio and video technicians. Except for the camera operators, most of the team works in a control room full of television monitors, video and DVD replay machines, and power sources.

Unless you're working in one of the few stadiums that still have hand-operated scoreboards, you'll need to be skilled in using audio and video technology. Baseball's Atlanta Braves, for example, use custom-designed software to help run their 5,600-square-foot (520 square meters) main scoreboard. The technology brings high-definition video, animation, and custom graphics to the scoreboard's giant video screen. Before the software can provide statistics, lineups, out-of-town scores, and even scorecard display graphics to various scoreboards around the stadium, scoreboard operators need to supply the system with all such information. Many new ballparks and

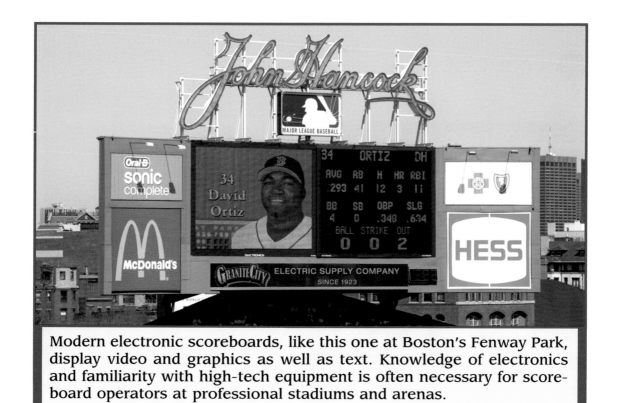

Modern electronic scoreboards, like this one at Boston's Fenway Park, display video and graphics as well as text. Knowledge of electronics and familiarity with high-tech equipment is often necessary for scoreboard operators at professional stadiums and arenas.

arenas employ similarly high-tech systems. Even the most user-friendly of these systems takes some initial training and previous technical know-how to be operated properly.

Scoreboard operators also need to have a thorough knowledge of the game so that graphics and information displays are both appropriate and synchronized to the game situation. Concentration and accuracy are essential. Operators working on manual scoreboards, like those found in older baseball stadiums, usually work in two-person teams and do a fair amount of heavy lifting as the large tiles can be quite cumbersome.

Work is primarily done at night and on weekends and holidays. The hours can be long: scoreboard operators for

Sony Open in Hawaii

This scorekeeper posts the final score for professional golfer Vijay Singh at the 2005 Sony Open in Honolulu, Hawaii. Career prospects at golf courses—even the biggest ones—are slim since volunteers often operate scoreboards in exchange for playtime on the course.

the top professional leagues arrive hours before game time to review the day's show plans and make sure everything's working properly. The number of work days vary, especially in the NFL. Giants Stadium, for example, hosted fewer than forty events in the second half of 2004, and that's with two NFL teams calling it home. Baseball stadiums host eighty-one home games but are rarely used for other events. In the NBA, teams have forty home games. Basketball arenas also frequently host tournaments, concerts, and conventions. But even the busiest venues use their scoreboards fewer than 200 times a year.

Education and Training

Some technical training is necessary for electronic scoreboards. Vocational high schools offer courses in electronics, but for the

Hands-Free Operation

The basketball scoreboard at the University of North Florida might be the world's only scoreboard that's operated completely hands-free.

Kenton Bell, the scoreboard operator, was born without arms or legs, but that hasn't stopped him from fulfilling his dream. Using a metal rod that he holds in his mouth, Bell has been a college basketball scoreboard operator for about twenty years. It all started during his sophomore year at the University of Kentucky, when the coach of the Wildcats' wheelchair basketball team asked him to work the scoreboard. Using his nose and his chin, Bell got the job done. "The switches were on different

(continued on the following page)

Kenton Bell displays the technique that allows him to operate the University of North Florida basketball scoreboard despite having been born with no arms or legs. "Working with the rod in my mouth is like a person with one finger," Bell explains. "I can do with one finger what most people cannot do with two hands and a finger."

(continued from the previous page)
sides of the control panel, so I had to move from side to side and do it quick enough so I could keep up," Bell told the *Jacksonville Times-Union*. "I got used to it, got the rhythm down and no problem. I knew exactly from that moment on what my calling would be in athletics."

Source: http://www.ncaa.org/news/2002/20020304/endzone.html

higher levels and bigger venues, continuing-education courses or even an associate's degree is usually necessary.

Like many sports jobs, the best way to get started is by working at the lowest levels. That often means volunteering at youth leagues or golf courses, or working part-time at a high school. In many high school and smaller college programs, the scoreboard operator also functions as the game's official scorer. Even the biggest, most well-known golf courses generally rely on volunteers to update the leader boards and record the progress of an event in exchange for playing on the course and being among the first to know how every player is performing.

With some experience and training, you'll be able to work at small colleges. The job is still usually part-time, but the equipment is more advanced. From there, the most talented and dedicated can move on to major college and professional programs.

Mr. Scoreboard

Louis J. Adamie, known to many as Mr. Scoreboard, was one of the most well-known and longest-tenured scoreboard operators. As a teenager in 1940, Adamie entered the old St. Louis Browns' Sportsmen's Park and was hired as the team's scoreboard operator. He spent the next forty-one seasons recording every hit, run, and error in more than 4,000 games, first for the Browns and then the St. Louis Cardinals in Busch Stadium. Adamie worked the scoreboard for seven World Series and five All-Star Games, retiring after the Cardinals won the 1982 World Series. In the 1950s, he became one of the first scoreboard operators in the country to run an animated display board. He won many honors, including a Baseball Writers Association of America award and induction into the St. Louis Sports Hall of Fame. In 1968, he became the first (and still the only) scoreboard operator to be honored in the National Baseball Hall of Fame.

Salary

Most part-time scoreboard operators at high schools and smaller colleges are either volunteers or get paid hourly—anywhere from minimum wage to about $9 an hour. Some operators are paid by the game. Public schools in the city of Virginia Beach, for example, paid scoreboard operators $20 per game for the 2004–2005 school year. Most colleges with big athletic programs pay between $30 and $100 per game.

Outlook

Part-time jobs at high schools and colleges are abundant. Competition for full-time jobs at major college athletic programs and professional leagues can be fierce. As a result, many scoreboard operators hold on to their jobs for numerous years, and job openings can be scarce. Nevertheless, new professional leagues have recently started in many sports, increasing the number of job opportunities. The more training and experience you have, the better your chances will be.

FOR MORE INFORMATION

ORGANIZATIONS
Information Display and Entertainment Association (IDEA)
1990 East Lohman Avenue, Suite 126
Las Cruces, NM 88001-3116
(888) 832-4332
Web site: http://www.ideaontheweb.org
 An international association of electronic display system and
 scoreboard operators that represents teams, public facilities,
 manufacturers, and suppliers worldwide.

WEB SITES

Daktronics
http://www.daktronics.com
> Leading manufacturer of scoreboards and scoring tables for professional and college venues.

DiamondVision
http://www.diamond-vision.com
> The originator of large-screen video displays.

BOOKS

Houseman, Randy. *The Golf Professional's Complete Guide to Scoreboards.* Eagle, CO: Green Grass Publications, 1999.
> This book teaches golf professionals the art of developing and presenting tournament scoreboards, including sections on layout, presentation, scoring, and more.

Nowlin, Bill, and Cecilia Tan, eds. *The Fenway Project.* Cambridge, MA: Rounder Books, 2004.
> Sixty-one of baseball's most ardent and knowledgeable fans contribute essays on one night on the field, in the stands, and behind the scenes at Boston's Fenway Park. Includes an essay by Eric Enders on the two men who operate the ballpark's manual scoreboard.

PERIODICALS

Pro AV
7015 College Boulevard, Suite 600
Overland Park, KS 66211
(913) 469-1185
Web site: http://proav.pubdyn.com
> A monthly magazine featuring news and articles on emerging technologies, as well as offering tips and techniques for audio-visual professionals.

5

OFFICIAL SCORER

If you enjoy keeping score when you go to sporting events, know the rules inside and out, have a high level of communication, are good at making quick decisions, and think you can handle the criticism that inevitably follows those decisions, official scorer might just be your dream job.

Description

Even at the highest levels, being an official scorer is essentially a part-time job. Most official scorers are either retired or have other jobs in addition to scorekeeping.

Every sport has official scorers, but the particulars of the job differ from sport to sport. The basic duty of the scorer, however, is always the same: to record every action in the game. Hockey scorers record all goals and assists, including the time each goal is scored. Basketball scorers record field goals, attempts, assists, fouls, and every other in-game statistic. Baseball scorers record the action in great detail, too; they compile box scores, which are abbreviated summaries of the game's main statistics. However, far from being mere transcribers, it is the scorer's discretion that determines hits and errors, wild pitches and passed balls. In certain situations, they award wins and saves to pitchers.

In many high school and smaller college athletic programs, the official scorer also serves as timekeeper and sometimes even scoreboard operator. Official scorers never go on the field during a game. They typically watch from the press box or scorer's table. Baseball scorers in professional leagues usually have a television nearby for watching replays and a microphone for announcing decisions on questionable plays. Most teams have one main scorer who works anywhere from

Just try to get a seat with a better view of the game than what Herb Turetzky, the New Jersey Nets' official scorer, has here at an NBA Finals game. Turetzky has been scoring Nets games since the team came into existence in 1967.

about 40 to 60 percent of the team's games, and one or two alternates who fill in the rest of the time.

A typical workday for a professional game scorer begins about an hour before game time. Most survey the lineups and begin filling in their scorecards, and the more thorough baseball scorers even examine the field to see if they'll need to adjust their judgments based on its conditions. After each game, most official scorers are responsible for sending a detailed report to statistics organizations and an official record of the game to the league.

Even at the highest levels, there's generally no travel involved, unless you are selected to score an All-Star game or postseason games. Playoff games in most professional leagues usually have a team of at least three official scorers who all confer on scoring calls.

Most sports have a specific set of rules for official scorers. These rules outline scorers' duties and indicate how they should use the rules of play in their scoring. Major League Baseball may have more complicated and comprehensive rules than any other sport. More than a quarter of their ninety-seven-page official rule book is devoted to scoring!

Knowing the rules is the main requirement of the job, but it's not the only one. Official scorers need integrity, a high level of concentration, and confidence in their judgment. Especially in baseball, there are situations in almost every game where a scorer's judgment can affect the statistics of several players. And as you might imagine, players can be protective of their statistics. Offensive players want to be credited with hits to help their batting averages, defensive players want their errors to be called hits to protect their fielding percentages, pitchers want hits to be called errors to lower their earned run averages, and managers want to defend their players. Fans and even broadcasters can be tough critics when they disagree with the official scorer. You must be able to stand your ground when you know you've made the right call.

In fact, many professional baseball players have been known to find the official scorer after the game in order to

Official scorers make decisions that can affect the statistics of several players at once. Here, Cleveland Indians catcher Victor Martinez tries to catch a wild pitch as Oakland Athletics baserunner Marco Scutaro scores an unearned run.

protest a call that didn't go their way. Chaz Scoggins, a long-time official scorer for the Boston Red Sox, made it onto ESPN's highlight reel when he reversed his own call and changed an error to a hit late in the 1992 season. The change credited two more earned runs to Boston's Roger Clemens, who was contending for the league's earned run average title at the time. Scoggins has also said that he still receives criticism for a call he made in the 1986 World Series on a wild pitch that many fans apparently continue to think should have been a passed ball.

Education and Training

Being an official scorer requires no formal training. There are no courses in scoring, and no exam to take to become certified. You do need to know the rules of the game backward and forward. A good way to get started is to work as a scorer for a college or minor league team. The minor leagues are not officially a training ground for scorers, but they are a good way to get experience and get noticed by a major league team.

Official scorers come from all backgrounds and vocations. The scoring for the New York Mets and Yankees, for example, is done by a group of four primary scorers: a retired sports reporter, a retired newspaper editor, a part-time radio broadcaster, and a banker. Other teams hire high school coaches, accountants, or even postal workers. For Major League Baseball, anyone who's interested simply has to contact the commissioner's office. They research your baseball background and decide whether to have you shadow a scorer during games to learn the ropes. If the scorer thinks you're capable, he'll recommend that you be hired.

Salary

Official scorers are hardly in it for the money. High school positions tend to be either volunteer or minimum wage. Some programs do pay a bit more, especially if scorers perform additional duties. A YMCA in Chicago, for example, was recently advertising an opening for a part-time score-keeper/announcer at $8.50 an hour. Major college athletic programs and minor league teams pay anywhere from $30 to $100 per game. Major League Baseball pays $130 per game.

Outlook

High schools and recreational leagues are always looking for scorers, especially those who can perform other duties as well, such as operating the scoreboard or making public address announcements. Jobs in professional leagues are much harder to come by. However, many of the current generation's official scorers for Major League Baseball will be retiring over the next decade, and the league is frequently looking for talented, qualified alternates.

FOR MORE INFORMATION

ORGANIZATIONS

Baseball Writers' Association of America (BBWAA)
Web site: http://www.baseballwriters.org
 The original source of baseball's official scorers, the BBWAA is still responsible for electing players to the National Baseball Hall of Fame, as well as granting other awards.

WEB SITES

The Baseball Scorecard
http://www.baseballscorecard.com

This site includes a scoring tutorial, a glossary, links to other scoring resources, and a message board. It's a good place to get answers to some of the trickier scoring questions.

Baseball Scorekeeping and Statistics
http://members.tripod.com/~frank_eak/bbscore
An amateur site that provides scorekeeping definitions and explains various techniques. Also covered are rules for different levels of play and formulas for computing various statistics.

Major League Baseball (MLB)
http://mlb.mlb.com/NASApp/mlb/mlb/official_info/official_rules/official_scorer_10.jsp
This section of the MLB Web site contains all rules pertaining to official scorers.

The Official Scorer
http://www.officialscorer.com
A Web site that offers software for keeping score at all types of games.

BOOKS

Dickson, Paul. *The Joy of Keeping Score: How Scoring the Game Has Influenced and Enhanced the History of Baseball.* New York, NY: Walker and Co., 1996.
This book provides scoring techniques and nuances, as well as a history of scoring. It also includes discussions with official scorers, profiles of some famous people who enjoyed scorekeeping, and pictures of scorecards from historic games.
Lerner, Mark. *Careers in Basketball.* Minneapolis, MN: Lerner Publishing Group, 1983.
The position of official scorer is one of fifteen basketball-related careers described in this book.

Odums, R. I. *Career Guide to Becoming a Sports Statistician, Scorer or Official Timer.* Cleveland, OH: Guidepost Publishers & Distributors, 1986.
An informative guide for getting your career started.
Ramzel, Carter, and Lee Tunnell. *Keeping Score: A Baseball Handbook.* Round Rock, TX: Austin-Greystone Press, 1994.
This book uses a fictional game to illustrate scoring techniques for both routine and unique plays that can occur during a baseball game.
Wirkmaa, Andres. *Baseball Scorekeeping: A Practical Guide to the Rules.* Jefferson, NC: Macfarland & Co., 2003.
This detailed guide explains the rules of official scorekeeping, including the duties of official baseball scorers, scorers' reports, and scoring quirks such as substitutions, out-of-turn batters, and called and forfeited games.

6

CAMERA OPERATOR

If you like watching sports on TV, you've probably noticed all the different camera angles through which television broadcasts bring you the action, the instant replays, and the pre- and postgame interviews. All of that coverage is possible because of the work of skilled television camera operators.

It can be as important for a camera operator to get into position quickly as it is for a referee. Seattle SuperSonics guard Luke Ridnour *(above)* fell into a television cameraman during a 2005 NBA playoff game against the San Antonio Spurs.

Description

The basic duty of camera operators is to record events for the fans watching at home. It is often exciting: whether they're filming a game-winning goal or touchdown, or a photo finish at a race, camera operators are witnesses to history.

Professional TV broadcasts have large camera crews, with each crew member assigned to a specific location or camera angle. Some camera operators stay in one place and shoot whatever passes in front of their lens. For example, some sit in a camera well right alongside the field of play, or they might operate stationary cameras three or four stories above centerfield during baseball games. Most sports broadcasts have at least one stationary camera operator and have several mobile cameras in other positions. Sometimes, operators sit in cranes and follow the action while crane operators move them. Steadicam operators (like those on the sidelines at a football game or on the field during a postgame victory celebration) wear a harness to carry the camera and steady the picture while they move about the action.

Regardless of where they're stationed, operators set the camera position or mount before the event begins. They also adjust the camera controls for distance and lighting. And once they've filmed the action, operators view film to be sure they have the desired effect. Then they make adjustments if needed. Some operators may edit footage on the scene and relay it to the TV station.

Hours can be long and irregular. For example, if you are a camera operator for the TV broadcasts of a team sport, you will travel to all the team's road games, and you will work before, during, and after games, including nights and weekends. Camera operators for individual sports such as tennis or golf will travel to tournaments across the country and around the world to bring the action back home to the local viewership.

It may seem obvious, but it is important for sports camera operators to have solid knowledge of the sports they're covering. They must choose and present interesting material and react to unfolding events on the field. That means intense concentration. Missing a crucial play while focused on the wrong player or the wrong part of the field results in confused, angry viewers.

Perhaps the most important requirement, however, is technical expertise, both in equipment and filming techniques. Camera operators must know which film, lenses, lighting, and camera angles to use. They might be required to set up cameras and lighting equipment, plan shots, take measurements, and perform basic maintenance and repairs on the equipment. Camera operators must also stay up to date on the ever-changing technologies used in television broadcasts.

Camera operators should have a good visual sense. In addition, imagination, creativity, and, of course, excellent eyesight are important. Good verbal skills are needed in order to communicate with directors and technicians. Operators must also be able to hold or control a camera for long periods of time. Otherwise, the images will be unsteady.

Education and Training

People in the field can't seem to agree on the best way to get started. "If you ask 10 or 100 different people how they got

Focusing In

In addition to specializing in the type of subject they film, camera operators for film and television broadcasts often become experts in any of the many steps and processes involved in a large project:

- **Cinematographers or directors of photography** direct the lighting, help frame shots, and in general make sure that the look and feel of the film are in keeping with the director's vision.
- **Camera operators** control the camera, following the director's and director of photography's instructions. They are responsible for keeping the action in frame and responding to the action as it unfolds.
- **Steadicam and Glidecam operators** work with camera stabilization devices that combine the image steadiness of a dolly with the freedom of movement of a hand-held shot. They are used for camera shots in places where moving the camera is difficult or impossible.
- **First assistant cameramen** are responsible for the general maintenance of a camera. They change lenses, maintain focus during shots, mark the spots

(continued on the following page)

(continued from the previous page)

where people will stand, and measure the distance between the camera and the subject matter.

- **Film loaders** are in charge of loading and unloading a camera's film magazines and keeping the loading room in good, clean condition.

into this business you'll get as many different answers," says Chuck Barbee, a veteran director of photography. Some camera operators believe that a bachelor's degree from film school is the foundation for success. Others argue that unless you attend one of the top programs, a degree won't be of much help. Some sort of formal training is usually necessary, however.

Career and technical education programs in television production are available in some high schools. Many community and junior colleges and vocational/technical institutes offer courses in camera operation and videography. Some schools not only teach filmmaking but also provide opportunities for work experience. Reading up on the craft is important, whether that means books, magazines, or newsletters, to help you keep current with the technology and the industry.

Everyone seems to agree that hands-on experience is crucial. It helps you learn the craft and develop your skills, and it

Steadicam operators wear specially designed equipment to allow them mobility while keeping the image steady. This Steadicam operator takes a quick drink through his masked helmet on the sidelines of a professional football game.

gives you the all-important "demo tape" that employers will want to see. Check whether your school offers internships with local production companies. Summer or part-time employment with cable and television networks, movie studios, or even camera and video stores is also helpful. As long as you're making contacts and learning the craft, any related experience will be worthwhile.

Salary

As with most careers, salaries vary by employer and by the camera operator's skill and experience. The majority of camera operators earn somewhere between $20,000 and $57,000 a year. The lowest earners make around $14,000 to $16,000, while those at the top of the field earn $65,000 and up. For those paid by the hour, 2005 data from the U.S. Department of Labor shows median hourly wages to be $18.50, with half of all camera operators earning between $11 and $28 per hour.

Outlook

Camera operators can be employed by independent television stations, large television and cable networks, local network affiliates, or independent production companies. It's a specialized profession, but with leagues expanding to new cities, an increasing number of sports networks, and Internet broadcasts growing in popularity, opportunities should increase somewhat over the next several years. As more TV stations and networks start broadcasting in high definition, camera operators familiar with the technology will be in greater demand. The majority of jobs, as well as the best-paying jobs, tend to be in large urban areas, where there are more television viewers.

FOR MORE INFORMATION

ORGANIZATIONS

National Association of Broadcast Employees and Technicians
501 Third Street NW
Washington, DC 20001
(800) 882-9174
Web site: http://www.nabetcwa.org
   This is the broadcast and cable television workers' sector of the Communications Workers of America, a national union.

Society of Camera Operators
P.O. Box 2006
Toluca Lake, CA 91610
(818) 382-7070
Web site: http://www.soc.org
   A nonprofit organization representing camera operators, camera assistants, photography directors, and other camera crew members.

Steadicam Operators Association
5 Waterford Court
Monroe Township, NJ 08831
Web site: http://www.steadicam-ops.com
   This organization, formed by the inventor of the Steadicam, conducts workshops and produces manuals. Its Web site also offers job listings and other resources.

WEB SITES

Ron Dexter.com
http://www.rondexter.com/professional/production/shooting_sports _and_action.htm

A veteran with forty years of film and video experience offers advice on camera work for several different sports.

TV Cameramen.com
http://www.tvcameramen.com
This comprehensive site includes articles, equipment reviews, and message boards, plus links to schools and television stations.

TV Jobs
http://www.tvjobs.com
An Internet-based employment service for people looking for all types and levels of television work.

BOOKS

Carlson, Sylvia E., and Verne Carlson. *The Professional Cameraman's Handbook.* 4th ed. Boston, MA: Focal Press, 1993.
A book that teaches basic procedures and troubleshooting techniques and details the components and use of widely used film cameras.

Elkins, David E. *Camera Terms and Concepts.* Boston, MA: Focal Press, 1993.
This book contains definitions and illustrations of the terms and concepts every camera operator should know.

Hart, Douglas. *The Camera Assistant: A Complete Professional Handbook.* Boston, MA: Focal Press, 1995.
A comprehensive technical guide for camera assistants. Includes personal anecdotes from the author's years in the business.

Kenney, Ritch, and Kevin Groome. *Television Camera Operation According to Ritch.* Burbank, CA: Tellem Publications, 1987.
Industry veteran Ritch Kenney offers advice.

Millerson, Gerald. *Television Production.* 13th ed. Boston, MA: Focal Press, 1999.

With more than 1,000 illustrations and diagrams, this technical bible for television producers goes into great depths on many aspects of production.

Zettl, Herbert. *Television Production Handbook.* 9th ed. Belmont, CA: Wadsworth Publishing, 2005.

This best-selling textbook introduces the basic skills required in all aspects of television production, as well as the latest production methods and technology.

PERIODICALS

ICOM: Film & Video Production & Postproduction Magazine
Web site: http://www.icommag.com

A monthly online magazine covering all aspects of the film industry, including acting, camera operation, and makeup art.

The Operating Cameraman
P.O. Box 2006
Toluca Lake, CA 91610
(818) 382-7070
Web site: http://www.soc.org/magazine.html

A semiannual publication of the Society of Camera Operators.

7

EQUIPMENT MANAGER

Imagine your favorite team trying to play without any equipment: no uniforms, no custom-made athletic shoes, no padding, not even a ball. That would be a nightmare for any equipment manager, whose job is to make sure that, whether playing at home or on the road, all team members have everything they need to perform their best.

One of the toughest parts of an equipment manager's job is to organize and pack everything that the team will need for a road trip. Here, Indianapolis Colts assistant equipment manager Mike Mays packs up the football players' bags in preparation for a preseason trip to Tokyo.

Description

An equipment manager's job consists of two main duties: making sure players have the right equipment to keep them safe from injury during games, and coordinating so that every player has what he or she needs at all times. In a nutshell, equipment managers must think of everything and be prepared for every possibility. They are responsible for ordering, securing, organizing, maintaining, shipping, packing, and

Above, the Baltimore Ravens' assistant equipment manager Darin Kerns helps a player adjust his helmet during a practice session. Equipment managers occasionally go on the field during a game when their assistance is needed.

unpacking every piece of equipment the team's players use in practice and games. In addition to supplying players with any custom-fitted equipment and uniforms, equipment managers are also typically responsible for assigning lockers and uniform numbers.

Football players wear more equipment than just about any other athletes, so their equipment managers have more items to issue, track, and maintain. During a game, for example, every NFL player is protected by the following custom-sized items: helmet shell and inner padding, face mask, chin strap, mouth guard, shoulder pads, hip pads, thigh pads, knee pads, jersey, pants, gloves, and shoes.

It can be hard enough to make sure that each player has the necessary and proper equipment at home games. Road trips complicate matters significantly, and coordinating them can be like running a military operation. Impeccable organization and attention to detail are crucial. Equipment managers make sure every piece of equipment is labeled, packed, transported, and unpacked. They also need to be able to anticipate any possible problems. For example, outdoor sports teams must have extra gear for any kind of weather. That could mean warm jackets, turtlenecks, and portable heaters for players to keep warm; cooling fans, extra undershirts, and jerseys so hot, sweaty players can change into fresh clothes; and hundreds of pounds of rain gear in case of a downpour. They might have to pack several types of mitts for utility baseball players, different hockey sticks for power or agility, or various types of cleats for football or soccer players depending on the playing surfaces. And they need to have replacements on hand for when things break; NFL equipment managers replace ten to fifteen broken face masks every game.

Education and Training

In general, a high school diploma is all that is required to be an equipment manager. However, you'll also need to have knowledge of athletic, mechanical, and—especially for football—electronic equipment and supplies. Lifting and carrying

Packing List

Road trips are difficult for all sports equipment managers, but NFL teams travel with more equipment than just about anyone. According to HowStuffWorks.com, a packing list for an away game looks something like this:

- 53 player bags
- 40 coach and staff bags
- 20 personal luggage bags
- 4 football bags
- 1 extra jerseys trunk
- 1 valuables trunk
- 1 trunk of field equipment
- 2 rain-cape trunks
- 1 projector trunk
- 1 screen trunk
- 2 video printers
- 1 video-assembly trunk
- 3 camera trunks
- 3 tubes of camera tripods
- 3 empty camera bags
- 2 tape trunks
- 1 tent for video printer
- 1 coach-to-QB trunk
- 1 tool kit
- 1 headphone trunk
- 2 hotel trunks
- 2 orthopedic-device trunks
- 1 electrical trunk
- 1 emergency-crash trunk
- 1 air-mattress/ splint trunk

- 1 splint bag
- 6 10-gallon coolers
- 3 6-gallon coolers
- 1 folding table
- 9 clothes hampers
- 1 extra parts trunk
- 1 extra clothes/ pads trunk
- 4 extra equipment bags

For games in cold weather, the list gets even longer and includes skullcaps, thermal socks and underclothing, four kinds of gloves, muffs, handwarmers, cold-weather cream, and heated benches.

equipment requires a reasonable degree of physical strength. It is also useful to have basic tailoring knowledge so that you can fit players for uniforms and equipment and mend or alter uniforms when necessary.

Like most of the careers outlined in this book, the best path to success is to start local and work your way up to bigger teams and bigger leagues. A great way to get your foot in the door is to volunteer as the equipment manager for a local high school's team. Athletic programs at small colleges often employ part-time equipment managers. With experience, you can advance to jobs assisting the equipment managers at major college programs or professional teams, which in turn can lead to a job as a full-fledged equipment manager.

Salary

Small colleges pay about $10 an hour for part-time equipment managers. Major college programs pay around the same rate for assistant equipment managers. According to SportsCareers.com, equipment managers for professional teams earn $20,000–$50,000, with the average salary being $30,000.

Outlook

Equipment manager jobs are harder to come by than many of the other jobs detailed in this book. This is mainly because many teams at amateur levels don't bother to employ equipment managers. Instead, these teams require the players to handle all their own equipment. However, hundreds of professional teams and thousands of colleges have some sort of equipment manager positions available.

FOR MORE INFORMATION

ORGANIZATIONS
National Sporting Goods Association (NSGA)
1601 Feehanville Drive, Suite 300
Mt. Prospect, IL 60056
(847) 296-6742

Web site: http://www.nsga.org
> NSGA is the largest sporting goods association in the world and serves professionals in the sporting goods industry.

Professional Baseball Employment Opportunities (PBEO)

P.O. Box A
St. Petersburg, FL 33731
(866) 937-7236
Web site: http://www.pbeo.com
> This subsidiary of Minor League Baseball provides year-round job placement service to its member clubs and a career network for job seekers.

SGMA International

1150 17th Street NW, #850
Washington, DC 20036
(202) 775-1762
Web site: http://www.sgma.com
> A global business trade association of manufacturers, retailers, and marketers in the sports products industry.

WEB SITES

How Stuff Works

http://people.howstuffworks.com/fb-equip1.htm
> This section, entitled "How NFL Equipment Works," provides an in-depth look at the equipment and duties of an NFL equipment manager.

BOOKS

Easterling, K. E. *Advanced Materials for Sports Equipment: How Advanced Materials Help Optimize Sporting Performance and Make Sport Safer.* London, England: Chapman & Hall, 1992.

Jenkins, Mike, ed. *Materials in Sports Equipment.* Boca Raton, FL: CRC Press, 2003.
    This title provides a scientific look at the effects of materials technology on sports performance.
Mastroni, Nick. *The Insider's Guide to Golf Equipment.* New York, NY: Perigee Trade, 1997.
    Advice from several equipment professionals and a comprehensive directory including clubs, shoes, gloves, and rainwear.

PERIODICALS

Sports Edge
3650 Brookside Parkway, Suite 300
Alpharetta, GA 30022
(678) 297-3903
Web site: http://www.sportsedgemag.com
    A magazine focusing on sports equipment.

8

CLUBHOUSE ATTENDANT

Clubhouse attendants have access to athletes that few other sports careers can match. They spend time with them before and after games, become familiar with their likes and dislikes, know some of their darkest secrets, and sometimes act as sounding boards and unofficial therapists.

Description

Regardless of the sport, the location, or the level of competition, clubhouse attendants' jobs are pretty much the same. They are stock boys, gofers, chefs, launderers, maids, concierges, and personal assistants. They are responsible for washing uniforms, cooking, cleaning, and running errands—basically tending to the players' every need. Some clubhouse attendants even answer fan mail and sign autographs in players' names so that the players don't have to do it themselves.

No matter what they're doing, clubhouse attendants, informally known as "clubbies" by the players, are always on the move. The job requires dedication, a strong work ethic, organization, and attention to detail. They deal with a lot of different people every day, so clubhouse attendants need to be friendly and have good interpersonal skills, no matter what the circumstances. Discretion is important, too. There's an unwritten rule that what happens behind the closed doors of a clubhouse stays there. And, of course, clubhouse attendants should enjoy being around the game.

During the season, professional athletes often spend more waking hours in the clubhouse than they spend anywhere else, so a clubhouse attendant must make sure it is comfortable. Many clubhouse attendants deal with young players and therefore function as substitute parents. That can often mean listening to players' problems and offering advice, but most

One of the biggest perks for clubhouse attendants is getting to know the players well. "If they have a bad day, you stay away from them. If they have a good day, you're one of the boys," explains Mike Murphy, the long-time clubhouse manager for the San Francisco Giants. Murphy hasn't missed a home game since he began with the team as a batboy in 1958.

commonly it means stocking the clubhouse kitchen and pantry with the right food and making sure the players eat nutritious and appetizing pre- and postgame meals.

Attendants in golf clubhouses are responsible for the cleanliness and appearance of the clubhouse. They also usually respond to customer complaints and questions, rent and sell golf supplies to club members, receive greens fees, and operate driving ranges. In addition, attendants often maintain simple records, balance and prepare daily sales reports,

These golf bags are lined up outside the clubhouse of the Augusta National Golf Club at the 2005 Masters in Georgia. Golf clubhouse attendants are responsible for the cleanliness and appearance of the clubhouse, which often includes cleaning and organizing players' equipment.

order equipment from manufacturers and wholesalers, book reservations for tee times, and even monitor play on courses.

Professional sports teams at lower levels typically have just one attendant and a few part-time assistants. Higher levels may have staffs of ten or twelve, including one or two cooks. Regardless of staff size, however, the tasks are the same. On the day before the home team returns from a road trip, the clubhouse attendant will make sure everything is clean and organized, and will spend several hours shopping for food and supplies for both the home and visiting clubhouses.

The visiting team's bus arrives before dawn, and all the players' equipment and personal items (like family pictures or good luck charms) are unpacked and put into their lockers. Then uniforms must be washed—twice if stains don't come out the first time around. Just when that's done, the home team's bus pulls up, and the process begins all over again.

For a night game, the players will start arriving in the early afternoon, and clubhouse dues need to be collected from each player. The pregame meal should be set up so that you're free to get players whatever else they want. For example, you might pick up a player's family at the airport, drop off another's dry cleaning, tell a rookie how to get the utilities hooked up in his apartment, and recommend restaurants to players on the visiting team.

When the players hit the field for pregame practice, you'll clean the clubhouse again, grab something to eat, then restock the clubhouse refrigerator from the store room as necessary. You might be done in time to catch part of the actual game from the sidelines or the dugout. But before the game is over, you're back in the clubhouse preparing the postgame meal. Once the players go home for the night, you spend a couple more hours cleaning the clubhouse one last time and washing the newly dirtied uniforms. Sometime well after midnight, you can finally head home to get some rest.

As you might have guessed, clubhouse attendants put in very long hours. During a home stand, most attendants work at least sixteen-hour days, with the first and last day of each series being even longer because the visiting team's equipment needs to be unpacked when they arrive and packed up again before they leave.

USA Today ranked the job of clubhouse attendant as the sixth worst in all of sports. When considering the hours, the long list of job duties, and the stress associated with satisfying the needs of a few dozen athletes, it certainly doesn't sound very glamorous. But just try telling that to the people who do it every day. With unsurpassed proximity to the game they love, a team that becomes like a second family, and the knowledge that by performing their duties well they might help contribute to their team's on-field success, most clubhouse attendants will argue that they have the best job in the world.

Education and Training

The only education requirement to become a clubhouse attendant is usually a high school diploma. The best way to learn the job is to start at the bottom and move up to positions with more responsibility as you gain experience and skill.

For clubhouse attendants, starting out is usually at the part-time assistant level in local, semipro, or low-level minor league clubhouses. Many types of experience can help get that first job. For example, working as a gofer or a bellhop, or taking care of the needs of a large group of people in some other capacity can be a good first step. Working in a customer-service industry or any job where you've had to regularly create order from chaos can also be helpful experience. In baseball, sometimes batboys can double as clubhouse assistants or can move up to such positions. Once you get your first job as a clubhouse attendant, you can work your way up to bigger and higher-level teams.

Salary

Part-time clubhouse assistants at every level usually earn at least minimum wage, plus tips for running errands for players and coaches. Attendants for minor league baseball teams earn about $30,000–$35,000, including tips. They often supplement their income with other jobs during the off-season. The same job in a major league clubhouse can earn up to $100,000 a year with tips. Full-time clubhouse attendants also collect daily clubhouse dues from each player. Most of that money is used to purchase supplies and pay part-time assistants, but the clubhouse attendants keep whatever is left over.

Clubhouse assistants and attendants can make a lot of money in tips. Attendants for class AA (mid-level minor league) baseball teams, for example, average about $5,000 in tips per year. Tips at the major league level, where players earn much higher salaries, can be outrageous. It's not uncommon for major league players to tip $100 or more for errands like picking up pizza or dry cleaning. It's also customary for visiting players and managers to tip the clubhouse attendant when the team is leaving a city for the last time that season.

Outlook

Clubhouse attendants, especially at the highest levels, tend to stay in their positions so jobs open up very rarely. Assistant-level jobs are frequently available, however. Many clubhouse assistants are high school or college students who stay with the team for only a year or two until they graduate and move on to more conventional jobs in other fields.

FOR MORE INFORMATION

ORGANIZATIONS

Professional Baseball Employment Opportunities (PBEO)
P.O. Box A
St. Petersburg, FL 33731
(866) 937-7236
Web site: http://www.pbeo.com
   This subsidiary of Minor League Baseball provides a year-round job placement service to its member clubs and a career network for job seekers.

WEB SITES

Boston.com: Meet the Clubbies
http://www.boston.com/sports/baseball/redsox/gallery/
   09_02_05_redsoxclubhouse/
   See photographs of the Boston Red Sox clubhouse attendants in action, and make sure to click on the "Cleaning up" link to read the extensive accompanying article on what it is like to be part of the Red Sox clubhouse crew.

On Milwaukee.com

http://www.onmilwaukee.com/buzz/articles/migliaccio.html
This section of the Milwaukee daily online magazine features an interview with Tony Migliaccio, director of clubhouse operations for the Milwaukee Brewers.

The Anaheim Angels' Clubhouse Attendant

http://www.grandforks.com/mld/grandforks/sports/12062263.htm
An article about Brian "Bubba" Harkins, the visiting clubhouse attendant at Angel Stadium in Anaheim, California.

BOOKS

Ksicinski, Jim, and Tom Flaherty. *Jocks and Socks: Inside Stories from a Major League Locker Room.* New York, NY: McGraw-Hill, 2000.
A former visiting clubhouse manager at Milwaukee's County Stadium shares tales from behind clubhouse doors.

ARTICLES

Antonen, Mel. "10 Worst Jobs in Sports: Clubhouse Attendant." *USA Today.* May 20, 2005. Retrieved January 2006 (http://www.usatoday.com/sports/tenworstjobs-6-clubhouse.htm).
Don't let the title of this article fool or discourage you; it provides an interesting and thorough look at what is involved in a clubhouse attendant's job.

Smith, Willie T., III. "Bombers' Clubhouse Attendant Loves Being Around Game." GreenvilleOnline.com. June 3, 2005. Retrieved January 2006 (http://orig.greenvilleonline.com/news/sports/2005/06/03/2005060365543.htm).
An informative article about being a clubhouse attendant, focusing on the man who runs the clubhouse of a class A team in Greenville, North Carolina.

ZAMBONI DRIVER

If you're like most hockey fans, you've watched the Zamboni smoothing the ice and wondered what it would be like to drive one. In fact, so many fans have been curious about that same thing that some NHL teams have installed passenger seats in their Zambonis and started charging fans steep prices to ride along. Five hundred dollars can get a fortunate New York Rangers fan a ride

A lucky fan waves to the crowd during a World Cup of Hockey semifinal game in St. Paul, Minnesota. Many teams charge fans for rides on the Zamboni, but who wouldn't prefer to get paid by the team to drive it?

on one of the team's machines during a game. But forget about paying to ride one—the Rangers could be paying you to drive.

Description

Driving an ice resurfacing machine for a living can be fun, but the job entails a lot more than just 9-mile-per-hour (14.5 kilometers per hour) joy rides. In fact, the official job title usually includes words like "arena maintenance" and "ice technician." Zamboni drivers are typically responsible for maintaining the

Rink employee Greg Spadoni uses a dime to make sure he sharpened a level edge on a skate at the Riverside Skating Center in West Lafayette, Indiana. The best way to get your career started is to work at a local ice rink and learn the ropes from the more experienced employees.

Zamboni machine and all other ice-related equipment. In local rinks, the Zamboni driver might also be expected to clean and maintain the whole arena, sharpen skates, and work behind the counter renting skates and taking reservations.

Small arenas usually have just one driver per shift, but professional arenas often have an ice maintenance staff of ten to fifteen, including Zamboni drivers, snow shovelers, and people who pour hot water into the holes that hold the hockey goals (the hot water keeps the holes from closing up).

The actual ice cleaning and resurfacing takes about twelve minutes in local rinks and a mere four minutes between periods in the NHL. However, the hours for a full-time professional ice technician can be long. In professional arenas, ice workers often start early in the morning and work late into the night when the team is in town. Because the ice needs to be constantly monitored and cared for, workers must also show up when there's no game. Ice rinks that host concerts or double as basketball arenas require even more upkeep, and that can mean seven-day work weeks and frequent sixteen-hour days, very little of which is spent riding around on a Zamboni.

To prepare the ice for play, first everything that shouldn't be there—beer, hot dog wrappers, and whatever other trash—is removed from the ice. Depending on the arena and the previous night's event, this cleaning could take hours. Once that's done, the Zamboni can repair the ice's surface.

In addition to being able to watch every home game from a better-than-front-row seat, the biggest perk to the job must be the adoration that Zamboni drivers receive no matter what else is happening. The team may be losing and the players may be awful, but the Zamboni driver always gets cheered.

Education and Training

Most arenas require a minimum of a high school diploma or equivalent, and a valid regular driver's license. There are no schools or courses for driving ice resurfacers. However, drivers are expected to perform routine maintenance and basic repairs on the resurfacers and other arena machinery. Because of this, it can be helpful to take courses in refrigeration, plumbing, electronics, and auto repair. Such courses will help your on-the-job performance and will open more doors for you.

How A Zamboni Works

To leave perfectly smooth ice in its wake, a heavy blade under the Zamboni shaves a thin layer off the ice. A horizontal screw gathers the ice shavings and a vertical screw sends them into a large compartment that is contained in the front of the vehicle. If the blade is lowered too far, the compartment will fill up too quickly and overflow, shooting shavings back onto the ice. If it is not lowered far enough, too little is shaved off and nicks and rough patches are left in the ice.

Water is then fed from a tank to a squeegee-like tool, which smooths the ice. Dirty water is vacuumed, filtered, and returned to the tank. Finally, a towel behind the squeegee spreads clean, hot water on the ice. This hot water melts any remaining bumps and then quickly freezes, giving the ice a new, smooth surface.

Driving the ice resurfacer is only one aspect of a job that usually includes general maintenance of the ice and refrigeration equipment. Where multiple sports are hosted, stands and floorboards must be moved to convert the arena from one sport to another. Here, workers are transforming the Delta Center from the Utah Jazz's basketball court to the Salt Lake City Ice Arena.

Once you have a good understanding of the mechanics involved, the rest of your training comes on the job. Kenny Coyle, a Zamboni driver at New York's Long Beach Ice Arena, says that the best way to learn the ropes is to get a job at a local skating rink. That usually means seasonal, part-time work. Senior employees will show you how to drive the resurfacing machine and do everything else the job entails. The more you learn and the more useful you make yourself, the faster you can move up the ladder. With experience, ice maintenance technicians can graduate to bigger rinks and arenas.

Salary

At the lowest levels, work is often part-time and seasonal, with pay ordinarily in the range of $8–$12 per hour. Full-timers at local rinks usually earn between $17,000 and $20,000 a year. Wages in the NHL are hard to pinpoint, but ice workers at that level typically get paid benefits in addition to their salary, plus perks such as free tickets to games.

Outlook

There is no shortage of local ice rinks, especially in Canada and the northern United States. Because all these rinks need to be maintained, part-time and seasonal work should not be hard to find. Figure skating historically reaches its height of popularity during and immediately following each Winter Olympics so ice rinks are often busier and in greater need of paid help at those times.

Lower levels of professional hockey have enjoyed a bit of a renaissance recently as they became the only game in town because of the NHL lockout that eliminated the league's 2004–2005 season. However, the absence of NHL hockey for an entire year caused a decline in the sport's popularity that may take years to fully reverse.

FOR MORE INFORMATION

ORGANIZATIONS

Canadian Recreation Facilities Council
228 Main Street North
Moose Jaw, SK S6H 0G3
Canada
(306) 694-4447
Web site: http://www.crfc.ca
    This organization offers indoor sporting arena standards, a national arena census, and a forum for recreation facilities workers.

Ontario Recreation Facilities Association (ORFA)
1185 Eglinton Avenue East, Suite 402
North York, ON M3C 3C6
Canada
(416) 426-7062
Web site: http://www.orfa.com
    A Canadian nonprofit organization that offers its members professional development activities, information workshops, and a career service. The Web site includes the organization's suggested guidelines for refrigeration plant maintenance.

Serving the American Rinks (STAR)
1775 Bob Johnson Drive
Colorado Springs, CO 80906
(719) 538-1149
Web site: http://www.usahockey.com/star
A joint venture between USA Hockey and the United States Figure Skating Association to serve its members in the rink and arena industry. It runs training programs in ice maintenance and equipment operation, ice making and painting technologies, and basic refrigeration.

WEB SITES

Resurfice
http://www.resurfice.com
This company manufacturers Olympia ice-resurfacing machines.

Salary.com: Dream Job: Zamboni Driver
http://salary.com/careers/layouthtmls/crel_display_Cat10_Ser213_Par315.html
This Web page provides an in-depth look at the keeper of the ice at Joe Louis Arena, home to the Detroit Red Wings. Al Sobotka began working at the arena when he was in high school. Thirty years later, he still works at the arena.

Zamboni
http://www.zamboni.com
The company that created the first ice-resurfacing machine is still the most popular manufacturer. Its Web site features a history of the machine, an explanation of how it works, and links to Zamboni dealers.

BOOKS

Dossat, Roy J., and Thomas J. Horan. *Principles of Refrigeration*. 5th ed. Upper Saddle River, NJ: Prentice Hall, 2002.

A comprehensive look at the mechanical refrigeration cycle and associated equipment.

Stocker, Wilbert F. *Industrial Refrigeration Handbook.* New York, NY: McGraw-Hill Professional, 1998.
This book includes coverage of the fundamentals, design, installation, and operation of industrial refrigeration systems.

ARTICLES

Bartus, Kristin. "Not Just a Tool of the Trade, the Zamboni Is a Hockey Icon." *Michigan Daily* Online. February 20, 1997. Retrieved January 2006 (http://www.pub.umich.edu/daily/1997/feb/02-20-97/arts/arts1.html).
This article from a University of Michigan newspaper provides an interesting history about ice resurfacing and some good tips about how to get a job as a Zamboni driver.

Hutchinson, Becca. "Ice and Cold—Prized Commodities at UD Arenas." University of Delaware Online. December 19, 2005. Retrieved January 2006 (http://www.udel.edu/PR/UDaily/2006/dec/icearena121905.html).
A particularly informative article about what constitutes doing a good job as an ice resurfacer.

Karchmer, Jennifer. "Rink Ride Ends with Smooth Finish: Zamboni Machine Driver Renews Ice." *Poughkeepsie Journal.* May 1, 2002. Retrieved January 2006 (http://www.poughkeepsiejournal.com/projects/on_the_job/bu050102s1.shtml).
This article provides a thorough look at the background, experience, and responsibilities of a Zamboni driver.

McMorrow, Paul. "Paul Lawrence: The Iceman Cometh." *Boston's Weekly Dig.* Retrieved January 2006 (http://www.weeklydig.com/index.cfm/fuseaction/Article.view/issueID/4cdadfbf-6928-48db-ba2a-cade0945026c/articleID/ff6e9548- 95a0-4fee-8716-98d3bbf92b84/nodeID/8ea67746-b4d9-4901-88ec-65210e243151).
This article describes a lot of the other responsibilities Zamboni drivers have in maintaining an arena.

10

TEAM MASCOT

When Robert Boudwin runs out onto the Houston Rockets' home basketball court during each game, the crowd cheers. He gives it his all and shows off his best moves. When the final buzzer sounds, he walks back to the locker room to thunderous applause, exhausted from a hard night's work but looking forward to the next game. Boudwin doesn't play for the Rockets, however—he's their mascot, Clutch the Bear.

Description

Every mascot's job is to entertain the fans, but each mascot's approach is as unique as its costume. Some mascots, like Gorilla of basketball's Phoenix Suns, wow the crowd with acrobatics, jumping on trampolines and doing midair somersaults while slam-dunking. Others, like baseball's famous Phillie Phanatic, drive funny cars and win over fans with silliness. No matter how it is approached, being a team mascot isn't an easy job, but it can be a lot of fun.

Baseball, football, and hockey mascots tend to spend most of their time interacting with fans—leading cheers, high-fiving, and signing autographs. NBA mascots spend more time on the court performing routines, and their "stage" is much smaller than those of the other sports. All that clowning around can be painful, too. The potential for injury or dehydration during stunts is part of the job, however. According to the Mascot Hall of Fame, mascotting is second only to men's gymnastics in injuries per hours of "sport" performed.

Mascots need at least a basic knowledge of the sport they're working in, so they know when to be on the field, court, or rink and when to stay out of the way. A mascot's job is to connect with the fans, and he or she must be able to perform with thousands of people watching his or her

every move. Creativity is a necessity, too, and the most-loved mascots are often the most original and inventive. Strength and endurance are also important. The job can be physically demanding, especially for baseball mascots who are performing mostly outdoors in up to 100-degree heat. Even the mascots who stay in air-conditioned arenas do a lot of sweating because the costumes are heavy and warm and few have good ventilation. "There's definitely a heat factor, and a lack of oxygen," explains Boudwin, who says that he generally limits his skits to twenty-five minutes at a time. Between routines, he has just enough time to towel off, change into a dry shirt, and hop right back into his Clutch costume.

A typical day for Boudwin during the NBA season might first include an appearance at a local elementary school, in which case he will wake up at 6:00 AM, load his costume and any necessary props into his van, and head to the school. His assistant will meet him there to help him set up. He will do one of his standard two-hour school shows and then break for lunch. After eating, he might perform at another gig or maybe spend some time writing a new skit. Then it is time to head to the arena for that night's Rockets

The Houston Rockets' mascot, Clutch the Bear, gets the crowd involved during an NBA playoff game against the Dallas Mavericks at the Toyota Center in Houston, Texas.

game. If he has time, he will practice his skits and moves before the game. At 5:00 PM, he will attend a pregame meeting with the rest of the entertainment staff. They review the game log and scripts, and block out who is set to perform at what times. He will be on the court performing before the game starts, again during the five timeouts in each half of the game, during the breaks between quarters, at halftime, and then when the game ends. Those performances include a mix of cheerleading, dancing with the Rockets' dancers, performing on-court skits, and signing autographs—all in a heavy costume with little ventilation.

On another day, he might be traveling to perform at the NBA All-Star Game or a celebrity softball game—Clutch has rubbed elbows with Jack Nicholson, Kevin Costner, George Bush Sr., Tiger Woods, Adam Sandler, and Nelly, to name a few.

Schedules for most mascots quiet down in the off-season. Unlike many of his colleagues, however, Boudwin has no off-season, because Clutch is not his only character. He is also the man inside Haley, the mascot for the Houston Comets, a WNBA team. Nonetheless, in addition to the 75 games he works for the two basketball teams, he still makes time for about 250 nongame performances throughout the year. Add the time he spends instructing new high school, college, and professional mascots at the mascot training camp he runs every summer, and Boudwin is one busy bear.

Even with such a hectic schedule, Boudwin, who is married, insists that being a mascot is a great job for people who are raising a family. "Mascots are usually working when everyone else isn't," he explains. Sometimes, there is office work like getting props or setting up skits, but the hours are mainly weekends and nights, leaving most days free for spending time at home. And best of all, he says, the hours are flexible because, with the exception of the team's games, you set your own schedule.

To keep a mascot's persona consistent, professional teams usually have just one performer with no backups or understudies. Mascots don't travel nearly as much as the athletes they work

When the New York Mets introduced Mr. Met in the 1960s, they became the first Major League Baseball team to have a mascot. Dozens of major league teams—and hundreds of teams in the minors—have since introduced mascots.

with, however, which is easier on families. Birthday parties, All-Star games, and celebrity events notwithstanding, mascots spend most of their time in their hometowns.

Most career mascots retire from performing at around age forty-five. At that point, some of them move into the team's front office, usually into positions like director of in-game entertainment. Many others open their own entertainment companies.

Education and Training

The mascots who specialize in gymnastic acts were all competitive gymnasts before donning their current furry uniforms. For the earth-bound, a handful of mascot schools are available but they are not necessary for success. Being a mascot for a college team is the most common stepping stone to the pros, but it's certainly not the only way in. Many jobs as corporate mascots, cartoon characters for local store appearances, and the lowest levels of the minor leagues require little or no experience.

Bob Woolf, the Phoenix Suns' Gorilla, got his job when he outperformed about 500 other hopefuls in an open tryout in 1988. Most top mascots, though, started at the lower levels and worked their way up. As they gain experience and hone their skills, the most talented and polished minor league mascot performers can move up to higher leagues just like the players do, and then, for a lucky and gifted few, to the top professional levels. Mascot performers can also move from one sport to another fairly easily.

Salary

Mascot salaries depend largely on the league, the team, the popularity of the character, your tenure, and how aggressively you market yourself for outside appearances. Professional mascots are usually part-timers who get paid a set fee for every game or event. Fees for most minor league mascots are in the $25–$50 range per game, although popular mascots can earn more. Mascots in the top professional leagues earn significantly more money. NHL, NFL, and MLB mascots can earn anywhere from $20,000 to $100,000 annually plus benefits. NBA mascots generally earn $50,000 to $200,000. Those figures typically include a base salary for in-game performances plus fees for additional appearances.

Nongame performances—which normally include corporate events, store grand openings, birthday parties, school visits, and even wedding proposals—can be a big source of additional revenue for mascots, bringing in anywhere from $50 to $1,200 per appearance.

Outlook

With character-based amusement parks opening every year and live shows featuring costumed incarnations of

Top mascots can earn up to $200,000 annually and now can be voted into the Mascot Hall of Fame. Mascots from many sports teams gathered in Philadelphia in August 2005 for the first induction ceremony. Inductees included the Phoenix Suns' Gorilla, the San Diego Padres' Famous Chicken, and the Philadelphia Phillies' Phanatic.

children's television characters gaining in popularity, low-level character work is becoming easier to find. There are literally hundreds of minor league mascots. In fact, there are three different mascots for baseball's class A South Bend Silver Hawks alone!

However, mascots rarely vacate their costumes, so openings are few and far between, especially at the top professional levels. NBA mascots tend to hold on to their jobs even longer than those in other sports.

FOR MORE INFORMATION

ORGANIZATIONS

The Mascot Organization

(877) 962-7268

Web site: http://www.mascot.org

This nonprofit mascot staffing and representation organization (mainly for entry-level and non-sports work) brings mascot actors together and helps them book appearances.

Professional Baseball Employment Opportunities (PBEO)

P.O. Box A

St. Petersburg, FL 33731

(866) 937-7236

Web site: http://www.pbeo.com

This subsidiary of Minor League Baseball provides year-round job placement services to its member clubs and a career network for job seekers.

Street Characters, Inc.

(888) 627-2687

Web site: http://www.mascots.com

Started by the first mascot to perform in the NHL, Street Characters offers training seminars and videos, and manuals for performers and mascot program administrators. Its Web site lists upcoming mascot auditions.

SCHOOLS

ProMascot

1600 Magnolia Bluff Drive

Gautier, MS 39553

(877) 640-8706 or (228) 497-5876
Web site: http://www.promascot.com
 Run by former Montreal Expos mascot Pierre Deschenes,
 ProMascot offers mascot training sessions two or three times a
 year in Alabama and Mississippi.

Raymond Entertainment Group
62 North Chapel Street, Suite 4
Newark, DE 19711
(302) 731-2000
Web site: http://www.raymondeg.com
 This group, started by former Phillie Phanatic Dave Raymond, runs
 a "boot camp" for performers of all levels. It also creates characters
 for college and professional teams and produces mascot events.

Signs and Shapes International
9988 F Street
Omaha, NE 68127
(402) 331-3181
Web site: http://www.signsandshapes.com
 This costume company coordinates the annual mascot training
 camp run by Robert "Clutch" Boudwin in Omaha, Nebraska, every
 summer.

WEB SITES

GameOps
http://www.gameops.com
 A sports entertainment industry Web site that includes a mascot
 resource page. Visitors can find out about available positions, chat
 with mascots, and get career advice.

Mascot Hall of Fame
http://www.mascothalloffame.com

Started by Dave Raymond, the original Phillie Phanatic, the Mascot Hall of Fame exists only in cyberspace for now. The eighteen mascots on its executive board plan to turn it into a brick-and-mortar hall of fame and museum.

BOOKS

Ahearn, Daren. *The Professional Mascot Handbook.* West Point, NY: Collart Enterprises, 1982.
This book provides advice for mascot beginners.

Fournier, Peter J. *The Handbook of Mascots & Nicknames: A Guide to the Nicknames of All Senior, Junior, and Community Colleges Throughout the United States and Canada.* 2nd ed. Lithia, FL: Raja & Associates, 2004.
This reference guide lists the athletic nickname and/or mascot of colleges and universities in the United States, Canada, and Puerto Rico.

Yarbrough, Roy E. *Mascots: The History of Senior College & University Mascots/Nicknames.* 2nd ed. California, PA: Bluff University Communications, 2005.
A history of how many college teams got their nicknames and mascots.

11

MEMORABILIA DEALER

If you're like most sports fans, you own at least one item that has been autographed by a professional athlete. Meeting a sports hero and getting his or her autograph is always a thrill. How would you like to do that every day? Hang out with famous athletes while they sign autographs. Pore over sports cards of your heroes or items that were used in legendary games. Share mementos of great moments in sports with other fans. Those pleasures are all in a day's work for a memorabilia dealer.

Description

Sports memorabilia is currently a billion-dollar industry that includes sports card companies, grading services that determine the memorabilia's condition, autograph dealers, price-guide publishers, online auction sites, and manufacturers of protective cases.

There are several ways to sell memorabilia professionally, but the first thing you have to do is know your sports and know them well. To be successful, you need to be aware of who the popular athletes are in each sport and who the next crop of stars is going to be. What kind of memorabilia dealer you become depends on your entrepreneurial spirit. Some memorabilia dealers go into business for themselves, either opening up a store selling cards and collectibles, selling merchandise online, or both. Their jobs entail obtaining merchandise, setting prices (the condition of an item is a big factor when determining its value), and interacting with customers. Store owners also advertise to get their names out and schedule in-store autograph sessions with players from local teams. Many store owners and small-time dealers also attend sports card and memorabilia shows and conventions. At these shows, dealers sell their merchandise to the hundreds—sometimes thousands—of collectors who attend.

At the other end of the memorabilia spectrum are large companies that specialize in autographs and game-used uniforms and equipment. These companies range in size but typically have many employees and more traditional office environments. A typical day might include setting up signings with athletes and their agents and selling inventory to wholesale clients. Some of these companies also buy inventory from other companies and stores or from individual collectors. Overseeing signings is one of the biggest perks because you spend time with athletes while they sign photographs, jerseys, and equipment.

Working for one of the established memorabilia businesses can often be easier than setting up your own. "It's very tough to start your own business," explains Ari Witkes of Grandstand Sports & Memorabilia, Inc., a company that specializes in autographs. When dealing with autographs in particular, Witkes says, "the biggest question is always authenticity, and by being with a major company you have instant credibility." The memorabilia business can also be a tough one to learn, so even if you plan to open a business of your own, it might make sense to first learn the ropes at a major firm.

Selling merchandise at memorabilia shows like this one can be an important source of revenue for independent dealers. Here, a large assortment of cards is displayed at the Sport Card and Memorabilia Spring Expo in Ontario, Canada.

A successful memorabilia dealer will also be outgoing and enjoy working with people, whether sports celebrities, wholesale clients, or individual customers. Dealing with athletes sometimes means dealing with egos, attitudes, and entourages, so the ability to stay cool under pressure will come in handy as well.

Q & A with a Pro

Ari Witkes is a vice president at Grandstand Sports & Memorabilia, Inc., a multimillion-dollar memorabilia company.

Q: HOW DID YOU GET STARTED IN MEMORABILIA?
A: I got an internship at Steiner Sports and then received a job offer at the end.

Q: WHAT ARE THE BEST AND WORST PARTS OF THE JOB?
A: The best is obvious—I am doing what I love: sports! You get to meet athletes and deal with them on a personal level. The hardest part is also dealing with the athletes and sweating over whether they will wake up on the wrong side of the bed.

Q: WHAT'S YOUR BEST ON-THE-JOB STORY OR EXPERIENCE?

A: I would say after the Yanks won the World Series in 1996, and we were doing signings with the team. They were all coming in at different times, and I got to meet my favorite team and celebrate with them. The player that sticks out the most is Derek Jeter. He is as classy as they come. He gets there to do the signing and—get this—he introduces himself to everyone by saying, "Hi, I'm Derek Jeter. What's your name?" I mean, really, you're Derek Jeter? Thanks for clearing that up! He is the opposite of many guys who come in with their cell phones on and their heads in their hands not even talking to anyone.

The New York Yankees' shortstop, Derek Jeter, signs baseballs and photographs at a memorabilia show in Orlando, Florida. Authenticity is the name of the game for dealers (and collectors) who specialize in autographed merchandise.

Education and Training

The only training required of a memorabilia dealer is to watch and know a lot of sports. There is no formal education or certification of any kind. However, because authentication and grading are becoming increasingly important parts of the industry, there is a growing need for memorabilia dealers to be educated about these issues. While some formal courses in forensic handwriting analysis are available, such training is not necessary for the average dealer. Most dealers simply need to become familiar with the more popular players' signatures to be able to spot obvious fakes. Industry publications contain helpful information on methods of forgery and detection, as well as the nuances of grading and the differences between the various grading companies.

The best way to get into the industry is to start small. That could mean selling some items online to get a feel for the business, or getting a part-time job in a memorabilia store. If your goal is to work for a major sports marketing and memorabilia company, the best thing to do is get your foot in the door with an entry-level job or internship. Once you're in, Witkes says, "do everything they ask and then some. Make yourself stand out and they will remember you when they are ready to hire. Any memorabilia company would rather hire someone who is familiar with their day-to-day operation than hire an outsider."

Salary

Salaries vary widely depending on the exact type of business you're in. Part-time jobs in memorabilia stores usually pay minimum wage. Some dealers sell memorabilia only part-time online. Others open their own memorabilia stores, where there is no floor or ceiling for revenues. Dealers in business for themselves earn salaries based entirely on how much they sell. Selling merchandise at sports card and memorabilia shows and conventions can increase revenue and widen a dealer's customer base.

Starting salaries at established sports memorabilia companies are typically about $25,000 to $30,000 per year. Earning potential is virtually unlimited because the larger memorabilia companies have revenues in the tens of millions of dollars. Those at the top rungs of such companies can earn well into six figures and even higher.

Outlook

Ever since the baseball that Mark McGwire hit to break the single-season home run record in 1998 was bought at an auction for over $3 million, the memorabilia business has exploded. Niche fields within the industry, such as sports-card grading and autograph authentication, continue to move into the mainstream. As the demand for sports memorabilia continues to grow, so should job opportunities in the memorabilia business.

FOR MORE INFORMATION

ORGANIZATIONS

Professional Autograph Dealers Association

P.O. Box 1729W
Murray Hill Station
New York, NY 10016
(888) 338-4338
Web site: http://www.padaweb.org

This international organization is limited to dealers of vintage (pre-1965) autographed material.

Universal Autograph Collectors Club (UACC)

P.O. Box 6181
Washington, DC 20044-6181
Web site: http://www.uacc.org

Founded in 1965, the UACC is a nonprofit organization for autograph collectors and dealers.

WEB SITES

Beckett.com

http://www.beckett.com

This Web site offers card grading, auctions, message boards, a marketplace, and a card-show calendar.

Collect.com

http://www.collect.com

This Web site for collectors in all fields includes news, articles, forums, and a marketplace.

BOOKS

Froloff, Bill. *Buying & Selling Sports Collectibles on eBay*. Boston, MA: Course Technology PTR, 2004.

This book explains how to start as a dealer, including taking and posting photos of merchandise, writing descriptions, and setting prices. The book also advises buyers on conducting research, online memorabilia searching, and making intelligent bids.

Williams, Pete. *Sports Memorabilia for Dummies*. Indianapolis, IN: Hungry Minds, 1998.

Discusses the finer points of memorabilia collecting for beginners, with a focus on collecting as an investment.

PERIODICALS

Autograph Collector

510-A S. Corona Mall
Corona, CA 92879
(800) 996-3977
Web site: http://www.autographcollector.com

This magazine contains collecting news, celebrity interviews, and signing event listings. It also offers articles on topics such as counterfeit detection and tips on collecting autographs from various professions.

Card Trade

Krause Publications
700 E. State Street
Iola, WI 54990
(715) 445-2214
Web site: http://www.krause.com

A trade journal for professionals in the trading card industry.

Sports Collectors Digest

F+W Publications Inc.

4700 E. Galbraith Road
Cincinnati, OH 45236
(800) 258-0929
Web site: http://www.sportscollectorsdigest.com
> Geared toward the more advanced collectors. Covers all aspects of sports memorabilia collecting, including trading cards, autographs, uniforms, and equipment.

Sweet Spot
816 Congress Avenue, Suite 1280
Austin, TX 78701
(512) 708-1999
Web site: http://www.sweetspotnews.com
> *Sweet Spot* focuses exclusively on vintage and autographed sports memorabilia. It includes news and feature articles, show calendars, and interviews with historic sports figures.

Tuff Stuff
F+W Publications Inc.
4700 E. Galbraith Road
Cincinnati, OH 45236
(800) 258-0929
Web site: http://www.tuffstuff.com
> The only multisport price guide. Each issue includes player profiles, in-depth articles on collecting, and the latest news on what is hot.

12

USHER

Stadium ushers spend the whole day on their feet, they rarely get to watch much of the game while they're working, the work is repetitive, and they often have to deal with drunk or disagreeable fans. Then again, the hours are great, "taking a meeting" means talking sports with fans at the game, and your "office" has a better view than just

Longtime usher Howard Purcell has been showing Cincinnati sports fans to their seats since 1937—first at Crosley Field, then Riverfront Stadium, and currently at Great American Ball Park. Here, he is working at a Bengals game against the Houston Texans in 2005.

about any other in the world. If you spend a lot of time at your local stadium and often find yourself pointing confused fans in the right direction, you might want to consider becoming a stadium usher.

Description

Ushers check ticket stubs and escort people to their seats. They answer fans' questions and point them to concession stands, restrooms, telephones, and ATMs. Ushers help fans enjoy their visit to the stadium in whatever way they can. At the lower levels of professional sports, they might also collect tickets from fans arriving at the stadium entrance or even sell refreshments during breaks. Ushers act as an additional layer of event security as well, monitoring the conduct of the crowd and either calming rowdy fans or having official security or police intervene when necessary.

The hardest part of the job is probably dealing with unruly fans. A good usher can usually settle fans down before a situation gets out of hand. However, that's not always possible, especially during tense games like playoffs or tournament finals when fans are already on edge or have had too much to drink and are not thinking clearly. Ushers sometimes have to enforce stadium rules and eject fans who become too disruptive, and because of their proximity to the crowd, ushers are often the first stadium employees to respond when violence erupts. They need to be able to assess a situation to determine the right course of action and need to know when they can handle a problem themselves and when they need to involve stadium security.

To be a helpful usher, you need to know the stadium inside and out so you can assist fans in finding their seats and everything else they need. You must also like working with people because the essence of the job is personal interaction. Successful ushers naturally enjoy helping people.

Don't Look Now...

Jerry "the Hammer" Smith manages the ushers and ticket takers at Boston's Fenway Park and is usually so busy during games that he rarely pays much attention to the action on the field. One evening, Smith asked a nearby fan for the score and thanked him by saying "God bless you, sir." The fan turned out to be the host of a highly rated sports radio show and was so amused by the exchange that he retold it on his show the next day, making Smith, however briefly, the most famous usher in Boston.

Ushers need to be exact in their work, or else they will end up seating one fan in another's seat or telling fans the wrong way to go. Good eyesight is important as well, so you can read people's tickets and notice any potential problems brewing in the stands.

Most ushers work part-time, showing up at the stadium shortly before it opens to fans. Some more-experienced ushers work longer hours and supervise other ushers, ticket takers, and various stadium personnel. Ushers work only during home games or local events, so there is no travel and plenty of time off. However, the majority of sporting events take place

on nights and weekends. Ushers don't usually interact with the players, but they have contact with players' families and friends, who frequently attend games. Ushers often receive free tickets to other events at the stadium or arena in which they work. In major league baseball, ushers receive the perk of free admission to every park in the league.

Education and Training

Training for ushers is generally done on the job. If you're having trouble landing a job at the sports arena of your choice, a good way to gain some experience is through part-time work as an usher at a movie theater, performing arts center, or amusement park. These types of venues frequently hire high school students and recent high school graduates. You'll learn venue policies, safety procedures, and how to properly greet patrons. The experience and knowledge you gain should help you find similar work at a sports stadium. Having contacts who work for a local sports team can also be a big help.

Salary

Wages vary by the size of the venue, the geographic area, and the level of experience and responsibility. Pay for ushers and ticket takers ranges from about $13,000 to $20,000 annually, and the median salary is about $16,000. For hourly workers, the median wage is just over $7 per

At smaller venues, ushers are often required to take on other responsibilities, such as taking tickets at the entrance or even selling refreshments.

hour, or $1,220 per month. Ushers frequently receive small tips when they help fans find their seats. Full-time workers often receive health benefits.

Outlook

Over 100,000 ushers and ticket takers currently work in the United States, and the U.S. Department of Labor expects 20,000 more to be employed by 2012. Jobs are plentiful. Large sports stadiums and arenas each employ several dozen ushers.

FOR MORE INFORMATION

ORGANIZATIONS

British Columbia Government and Service Employees' Union
4911 Canada Way
Burnaby, BC V5G 3W3
Canada
(604) 291-9611
Web site: http://www.bcgeu.bc.ca
> This labor union represents 60,000 Canadian workers, including stadium ushers.

Professional Baseball Employment Opportunities (PBEO)
P.O. Box A
St. Petersburg, FL 33731
(866) 937-7236
Web site: http://www.pbeo.com
> This subsidiary of Minor League Baseball provides a year-round job placement service to its member clubs and a career network for job seekers.

WEB SITES

Ballparks of Baseball
http://www.ballparksofbaseball.com/seatingcharts.htm
> This section of a Web site dedicated to baseball stadiums has seating charts for every stadium in the major league.

Stadiums of the NFL
http://www.stadiumsofnfl.com/seatingcharts.htm
> A sister site of Ballparks of Baseball, this site includes seating charts of all NFL stadiums.

BOOKS

Delaney, Kevin J., and Rick Eckstein. *Public Dollars, Private Stadiums: The Battle over Building Sports Stadiums*. Piscataway, NJ: Rutgers University Press, 2003.
  A look at the politics of building sports stadiums and the people affected by it.
Green, Daniel S. *The Perfect Pitch: The Biography of Roger Owens, the Famous Peanut Man at Dodger Stadium*. Coral Springs, FL: Llumina Press, 2004.
  Green recounts the life story of a well-known stadium vendor.
Noll, Roger G., and Andrew Zimbalist, eds. *Sports, Jobs, and Taxes: The Economic Impact of Sports Teams and Stadiums*. Washington, DC: Brookings Institution Press, 1997.
  This book examines the economic impact of new stadiums on the cities that build them, including the jobs created (and not created) by their construction. It includes case studies of several major and minor league stadiums.

GLOSSARY

aerating A process by which thin holes are poked into grass, allowing air and water to penetrate directly to the roots.

amateur draft Annual draft in which major league teams take turns selecting high school and college players. Teams then own the rights for one year to sign contracts with the players they selected.

authentication The act of establishing the authenticity of; proving genuine.

auxiliary scoreboard Any smaller scoreboard meant to supplement a stadium's main scoreboard. Auxiliary scoreboards are rarely capable of showing graphics or video.

camera well An area, not far from the action being recorded, where camera operators and their equipment are stationed.

cinematography The art or technique of movie photography, including both the shooting and the development of the film.

clubhouse The locker room of an athletic team.

contact Any physical touching between players of opposite sports teams. Certain types of contact are in violation of the rules and can result in penalties.

drainage A lawn or playing field's ability to drain moisture.

dues A charge or fee for membership, as in a club or organization.

earned run Any run that does not score as a result of an error.

ejection When an individual, usually a player or coach, is removed from a game by a game official for bad behavior.

error Any play during which a defensive player fails to make a routine play, resulting in a batter reaching base, a runner advancing one or more bases, or a batter's turn at bat being prolonged.

footage A series of camera shots of a specific nature or subject.

free agent A professional athlete who is free to sign a contract with any team.

game-used An item of memorabilia that was used by a professional athlete during a game.

gofer An employee who runs errands in addition to performing regular duties.

grading A system used to determine the condition of sports memorabilia, especially trading cards.

greenskeeper A groundskeeper for a golf course.

high-definition A designation of television picture and sound quality. High-definition video displays 1,080 lines of resolution, resulting in much crisper and more detailed images than those produced by the 480 lines of resolution inherent to standard-definition video.

magazine A compartment in a camera in which rolls or cartridges of film are held for feeding through the exposure mechanism.

memorabilia Objects valued for their connection with historical events, culture, or entertainment.

mount Any stand or set position for a television camera.

passed ball A pitched ball that eludes the catcher when at least one runner is on base and allows the runner(s) to advance. The catcher is not charged with an error.

persona The role that one assumes or displays in public or society; one's public image or personality, as distinguished from the inner self.

portal A Web site considered as an entry point for other Web sites, often by being or providing access to a search engine.

refrigerant A substance, such as air, ammonia, water, or carbon dioxide, used to provide cooling either as the working substance of a refrigerator or by direct absorption of heat.

rookie league The lowest level of professional baseball, one step below class A. Usually populated by players just out of high school or college.

shadow To follow or trail closely.

signing Memorabilia industry term for a live autograph session with an athlete or celebrity.

tenure A period during which something is held, usually a job.

tripod An adjustable three-legged stand, as for supporting a camera.

trunk A large packing case or box, used as luggage or for storage, that clasps shut.

turf A surface layer of earth containing a dense growth of grass and its matted roots; sod. Also, an artificial substitute for such a grassy layer, as on a playing field.

unearned run Any run that would not have otherwise scored if an error had not been committed.

video board A large television-like screen found in sports arenas. Video boards typically show pictures, graphics, and replays related to the action on the field.

videography The art or practice of using a video camera.

wild pitch A pitched ball that is delivered in such a manner that the catcher cannot catch it with ordinary effort. A wild pitch can only be called with one or more runners on base and only if it allows the base runner(s) to advance.

INDEX

About the Author

For seven years, Adam Hofstetter combined his love of sports with his bachelor's degree in creative writing by running an award-winning sports commentary Web site that was praised in *Sports Illustrated*, on CNN, and in dozens of magazines, newspapers, and sports radio shows throughout the United States and Canada. His writing has also appeared in the *2001 Big Bad Baseball Annual* and the online version of *ESPN the Magazine*. When he's not at Shea Stadium watching the Mets, Hofstetter can usually be found in Cedarhurst, New York, where he lives with his wife, Sarah, and their two children, Abby and Sam.

Photo Credits